THE AUTHOR

Catherine James was born in Sheffield, and spent part of her childhood on the West Coast of Scotland. Writing, especially poetry, has always been part of her life.

After a career in teaching, she now lives in Derbyshire. It is a county which she has come to treasure, and in which her travels have opened up a wealth of dramatic landscapes, ancient villages and lively towns.

On one such journey, she went to Wirksworth, on a mission for a friend to discover connections between the writer George Eliot and Derbyshire.

Here, near the market place, she found the bookshop owned by Richard Barrett. During the search for possible literature, the conversation turned to the many writers who had visited the area. Several of them, too, had referred to the county in their books and letters.

A lane near Ashbourne

So, the idea was born of exploring the references to the places in Derbyshire in the writings of the authors who had visited them.

Since that visit to the book shop in Wirksworth, Catherine's travels have now taken her to the villages and towns of the Peak District and Derwent Valley. At times, she has stayed in them, to gather impressions and information. Others have been revisited on many occasions, and at different seasons. All have been possible using public transport.

The travels and visits have been fascinating, as there has been so much to discover. But it has been the meeting with so many kind and interested people which has given the writer great enjoyment too.

This book, then, is a tribute to the people of Derbyshire as well as to the beautiful county in which they live.

Catherine James, Allestree, July 2018

DERBYSHIRE
WHERE WRITERS WALKED

CATHERINE JAMES

COUNTRY BOOKS

Published by Country Books
Courtyard Cottage, Little Longstone, Bakewell, Derbyshire DE45 1NN
Tel: 01629 640670
e-mail: dickrichardson@country-books.co.uk
www.countrybooks.biz

ISBN 978-1-910489-54-3

DEDICATION

David and Hope Haggan,
for all their love and care over many years

COVER PICTURES

Front: *Stanage Edge*
Back, top left: *North Lees*
Back, top right: *Bakewell*

Printed and bound in England by 4edge Ltd. Hockley, Essex. Tel: 01702 200243

CONTENTS

CHAPTER TITLES

ACKNOWLEDGEMENTS

The journey of the book began with researches into the places, – the houses, villages, towns and landscapes – which had possible connections with some of our writers. My studies soon led to a wish to visit the places themselves, to explore those which the writers would have known, and to see their setting in the County. Public transport has been very useful in my explorations, either for day visits or for longer stays in villages such as Bakewell and Hathersage. I discovered that the places mentioned in the book were all possible by bus or train.

During the years of my researches, though, it has been the people whom I have met on my travels, in churches, museums, hotels and cafés, who have contributed so much to my enjoyment in writing this book. Their kindness and interest have been invaluable, and without them, its completion would not have been possible nor such a delight. At the same time, I have corresponded with representatives of societies and associations, museums and libraries, and am greatly indebted to them for their support.

I would like to express my thanks to members of my family, my neighbours, and my friends both near and far away, who have travelled the road with me and given me such encouragement along its way.

I am especially grateful to –
Shain Bali, for the photographs of Derbyshire;
Richard Barrett, in whose book shop in Wirksworth, the story of the book began, for all his interest and encouragement during the journey;
John Burton, of The George Eliot Foundation, for his advice with reference to the chapter on George Eliot;
Breadsall Priory Marriott Hotel and Country Club, for the welcome during my visit and for kind permission to use of the photograph of

Breadsall Priory;
Sheila Griffiths of The Alison Uttley Society, for her encouragement and support with reference to the chapter on Alison Uttley;
Dorreen Milner from All Saints Church, Breadsall, for her kind welcome at the Church;
Robert and Christine Simpson of Rose Cottage Tearoom, Castleton, for their interest;
The New Matlock Bath Hotel, for the welcome during my visit and kind permission to reproduce the photograph of the Hotel;
The Peacock Hotel, Rowsley, for the welcome during my visit and kind permission to include photographs of the Hotel, including two of the interior by Tom Kahler;
The Rutland Arms Hotel, Bakewell, for the welcome during my visit. This was the first place which I visited for the researches and gave me the necessary encouragement at the beginning, to continue with them;
Richard Watkins, for his interest and support during my researches;
Professor Stephen Wildman, for his advice and interest with reference to the chapter on John Ruskin.

Finally, I would like to express my grateful thanks to my publisher, Dick Richardson, for all his kindness, support and encouragement, both during the journey of the book and at its conclusion.

PORTRAITS & PICTURES

JANE AUSTEN
Woodcut of Jane Austen, used in the 1870 'Memoir' by her nephew, by kind permission of Jane Austen's House Museum, Chawton.

CHARLOTTE BRONTE
1. Portrait of Charlotte Bronte, by J.H. Thompson 1850s by kind permission of The Bronte Society.
2. Engraving of drawing of Hathersage 1886, by T.C. Hofland.

ERASMUS DARWIN
1. Portrait of Erasmus Darwin by Joseph Wright c 1792-3, © 2017 Derby Museums Trust.
2. Full Street Derby pencil and watercolour by Peter Perez Burdett 1769 © 2017 Derby Museums Trust.
3. Photograph of Full Street, 1930s, by kind permission of Derby Local Studies Library.
4. Engraving of Breadsall Priory 1791 published by J Robson, New Bond Street, London.

DANIEL DEFOE
Engraving by Michael Vandergucht after Jeremiah Taverner 1706.

GEORGE ELIOT (Mary Ann Cross née Evans)
1. Replica by Francois D'Albert Durade 1849, National Portrait Gallery 1405, by kind permission of the National Portrait Gallery.
2. Portrait of George Eliot's Aunt Elizabeth Evans. By kind permission of Englesea Brook Chapel and Museum.

SAMUEL JOHNSON
1. Pastel portrait of Samuel Johnson, after Sir Joshua Reynolds, by an unknown artist. The original dates from 1756-7. By kind permission

of The Samuel Johnson Birthplace Museum, Lichfield.

2. Photograph of The Drawing Room of The Mansion House, Ashbourne (architect Robert Adam 1761-63), by H. Hinge 1932, by kind permission of Derby Local Studies Library.

3. Hand coloured engraving of 'Ashbourne Hall, the Seat of Sir William Boothby' c1850, published by Dawson and Hobson, Ashbourne.

JOHN RUSKIN

1. The High Tor near Matlock Derbyshire, engraving by Thomas Allom and J.W. Lowry, original 1836, hand coloured print c1845.

2. WA 2013.67 John Everett Millais, 'John Ruskin' © Ashmolean Museum, University of Oxford.

SIR WALTER SCOTT

1. Print by J. Graham, engraved by T. Woom, c1831 Fisher, Son & Co.

2. 'View into Hope Dale from Winnats', 1886, drawn by Sir Francis Chantrey, engraved by G. Cooke.

3. 'View from within Peake Hole near Castleton', 1886, drawn by Sir Francis Chantrey, engraved by G. Cooke.

ALISON UTTLEY

1. Cover of *The Private Diaries of Alison Uttley* edited by Denis Judd © Denis Judd , showing a portrait of Alison Uttley and drawings by Margaret Tempest

2. Photograph of Alison Uttley taken by her then fiancé James Uttley c1911 on Wimbledon Common, © The University of Manchester.

3. Hand coloured engraving of Cromford c1860, by Newman & Co, London, published by W. Bemrose & Son, Derby.

JOHN WESLEY

John Wesley by George Romney (1789) courtesy of The New Room, John Wesley's Chapel in Bristol.

John Wesley by John Michael Williams (1710-c1780), by kind permission of Lincoln College, University of Oxford, photographed by Keith Barnes.

THE JOURNEY CONTINUES

From the series of books, *The Beauties of England and Wales* engraving of Derby from drawing by H. Moore/James Greig c1805.

INTRODUCTION

Derbyshire is not Dorset.

There is no Thomas Hardy to conjure up the villages, and villagers, of Wessex.

No sisters have wandered its moors.

Beside the Derwent, no Bard has sung the love song of Juliet.

Yet writers have travelled through the County. Their books record memories of its mills and stone-hewn towns and rugged landscapes.

Some have paused. And the impressions they formed during their visits can be traced in descriptions of characters and places.

Others have lingered. They have put down roots. Their writings have often been a distillation of ideas and views developed over the months, or even the years, they spent in Derbyshire.

The hills of the area are honeycombed with caves. For centuries, from deep underground, lead and fluorspar and alabaster have been mined and quarried.

Its limestone has travelled across the land to construct roads or to be used in the manfacture of medicine. But to find the treasure, men have had to dig and delve. So, too, the snapshot pictures of Derbyshire are often hidden, tucked away in a paragraph of a book. Sometimes, the place-name has been changed. At others, the Derbyshire memory will be a piece in a mosaic, collected with many others from the writer's life.

The purpose, then, of this book is not to be a biography. Rather it is to serve as a companion-guide which can point the way to places which have inspired writers to tell the stories of Derbyshire.

It is as much to do with the places as with those who have written about them.

The visitors of today are invited to search for the buildings and landscapes found in the pages of literature, to linger, to be a detective and find the evidence for themselves.

For so much is waiting to be discovered in the hills of Derbyshire.

Pastel portrait of Samuel Johnson, after Sir Joshua Reynolds,
by an unknown artist, 1756-7
By kind permission of The Samuel Johnson Birthplace Museum, Lichfield

1. Following Doctor Johnson

TO DERBY

Every city, every town, has its own oases. A public park, a garden of flowers, a patch of grass with a shady tree can provide a place in which to pause for a while. Even a bench in a shopping centre, or a seat on a pavement set back from the road, give the opportunity for a moment's rest from the ceaseless movement of traffic and crowds.

Derby too has its oases. There are a number of beautiful parks, once the grounds of large houses, within less than a mile of its centre. But even at its heart, and often in unexpected places, hidden away among the walls, are breathing spaces.

One of these is at Cheapside. Here there are seats and a lawn. Daffodils in the Springtime, and fallen leaves in the Autumn create patches of sunshine, even on grey, cloudy days. It is good to spend a few minutes here, and to look around one, for Cheapside is surrounded by reminders of the history of Derby.

Roads radiate from this hub – their names recalling the city's long past. Echoes of Viking times survive in Friar Gate, Iron Gate, Sadler Gate – the word 'gate' being the Old Norse for 'street'. The name 'Wardwick' (the farm of a man called Walde) shows that a Saxon farmstead once stood there. Elegant brick and stone Georgian town houses line the wide avenue of Friar Gate. As we look up above the street-level shops, we are carried back across the centuries to the houses of local landowners, to welcoming inns, and brick and timbered craftsmen's homes. The past enters the present round every corner.

Behind Cheapside tower the stone walls of the Church of Saint Werburgh. Against the Church's foundations swirl the currents of the modern one-way system. Gales and floods have battered it. Walls have been repaired and rebuilt. But it remains – a reminder, amid so many changes, of the far-away origins of Derby.

Sadler Gate, Derby, looking from the Market Place towards St. Werburgh's Church

For the name of its patron saint, Werburgh, takes us back to the days of the Saxon kings. These were times of turbulence and warfare. But the gold and garnets of the Saxon Hoard speak of craftsmanship, of great wealth, and extended trade routes. Found in 2009 by a metal detec-

The Old Bell, Derby

torist in a field near Hammerwich, Staffordshire, and now considered to be the UK's largest and most highly-valued ancient treasure, it gives us a glimpse of the lives of the Saxon warrior elite. The 3800 pieces date from AD 600-650 and probably represent the battle spoils accumulated over decades of a powerful ruler.

This was an age, too, of the deepening spread and influence of Christianity. Rulers embraced the faith. Priests preached the Gospel beside stone crosses. Churches, monasteries and nunneries were established.

It was at the nunnery of Ely that Werburgh became a nun.

So who was Werburgh, or Werburga?

She was born about 650, at Stone in Staffordshire, and was a princess. Her father was Wulfhere, the first Christian King of Mercia, while her uncle was Paeda who founded Repton Church. Werburgh was drawn to the contemplative life, and wanted to devote herself to helping others. She took her vows at the Abbey at Ely, her life so full of humility, that it was said of her that to those in her care, she was more servant than mistress. After her father's death, her uncle King Ethelred invited her to found and oversee the nunneries in his kingdom. Communities of nuns were established at Hanbury and Trentham in Staffordshire, and at Weedon in Northamptonshire. It was here that the story of Werburgh and the geese originated. A flock of the birds was devastating the crops in the area, and so she 'commanded' them to leave, never to return. They wanted to obey, but their leader, called 'Grayking' had been killed & cooked by one of Werburgh's servants! Fortunately, he had kept the bones, which the Abbess miraculously restored to life, and so the geese were able to follow their leader away from Weedon. Such was her renown, that, after her death, she was venerated as a saint, often depicted with her geese as her symbol. Werburgh was buried within the Church at Hanbury, but because of the threat from Viking raids, her remains were removed to the Church of St. Peter and St. Paul in Chester. In 975, the Church was dedicated to St. Werburgh and St Oswald, and in the sixteenth century, became Chester Cathedral. Twelve churches have been dedicated to her.

The beginnings, then, of the Church of Saint Werburgh in Derby lie in this period. Derby was then called 'Northworthy', or 'North homestead'. According to the tenth century Chronicle of Ethelwerd, Northworthy was the name given to the settlement, "but it was Derby in the language of the Danes". 'North' suggests that it was related to an important Saxon site already in existence to the south – no doubt to

Repton. Perhaps the Church was founded as one of its mission churches.

The Cheapside area next to the Church, where we stand today, would be then have a space for trade. We can imagine a market and a small farming settlement, or 'wick', of wooden thatched huts where the trees now grow. Nearby ran the old Roman road. Beside the site flowed a brook, Markeaton Brook, now culvered over, and the River Derwent was not far away.

At the heart was the Saxon church, long since gone, but recorded in the Domesday Book.

There are several milestones in its history. After the Norman Conquest, the Church was given to Darley Abbey. Afterwards, its care passed to the Priory of Saint Mary in the Meadows, or Nuns Green. We know the name of its vicar in 1278 – a Walter de Markeaton. In 1359, Sir John Chandos founded a chantry, where Mass could be sung daily for the repose of departed souls. The tower was built in the late fifteenth or early sixteenth century, of which the lower parts survive. But the imposing tower under which we pause was rebuilt and extended in 1601.

After that, it is a story of wind and water doing their worst. The need for restoration was frequent, until in 1698, a great flood caused the partial collapse of the Church. It was rebuilt, reflecting the classical taste of the age, with a central dome, galleries, nave and chancel.

The chancel still survives, although the adjoining part of the church was rebuilt in the Gothic Revival style, in the nineteenth century, when the architect was Sir Arthur Blomfield. Its original carved woodwork, and a fine, wrought iron font cover by Robert Bakewell, remain. It is well worth a visit, not only for its history and furnishings, but as the setting for an event in the life of one of the greatest of Englishmen, Dr. Samuel Johnson. The chancel is now in the care of the Churches Conservation Trust. At the time of writing, its heavy old key may be obtained from the Derby Museum across the road. It is exciting to hear it unlock the wooden door and to pass into the chilly shadows of its interior.

For it was here, on July 9th, 1735, that Doctor Samuel Johnson married Elizabeth Porter, his 'Tetty'.

They had met three years earlier, in Birmingham, where Tetty lived with her first husband, a prosperous merchant called Henry Porter. The

St. Werburgh's Church, Derby

Porters had three children – two sons and a daughter. A portrait of Tetty, painted by an unknown artist in the early 1730s, has survived, described by her daughter as being "very like" her mother. It depicts her as a fashionably-dressed lady in a plain blue gown, with a direct gaze, blue eyes and fair hair worn simply in a long curl. Samuel obviously admired her hair, for he told Hester Thrale, a friend in later life, that it was "eminently beautiful, quite blonde like that of a baby". Some of Johnson's friends from the years when he had become famous, were less kind, describing her red rouged cheeks, and that she was short and plump.

The life of the happy family, however, into which Johnson was drawn, was not to last, for in 1734, Henry Porter became terminally ill. Johnson continued to visit his friend, and after Henry's death, to support his widow. The two grew close. Sometime in the months following her husband's death, she and Samuel decided to wed. Her children were divided in their response to their mother's second marriage. Her daughter accepted it from the beginning, one of her sons gradually being reconciled, but the other never doing so.

One reason for the family's reaction may well have been the age difference between Tetty and Samuel. On her wedding day, she was forty six and he was twenty five. They had married in less than a year after she was widowed. But another reason, too, must have lain with

St. Werburgh's Church, Derby, today

her choice of second husband. For until 1735, his life had been one of constant struggle, against illness, disability and poverty.

Samuel Johnson had been born in 1709, in Lichfield, the son of a book-seller Michael Johnson and his wife Sarah. Their home was a tall, imposing house overlooking the market place, and shows the aspirations of Michael, who had risen at one time, to become Sheriff of the city. It is now 'The Samuel Johnson Birthplace Museum', open to the public, and a fascinating place to visit with its collections of pictures, furniture and books devoted to Johnson and his times.

The prosperity, however, was not to last. Mr Johnson tried to diversify, travelling to sell his books, working as a small publisher, and marketing parchment. One of his journeys took him to Uttoxeter, to sell his books in the market place there. A reluctant Samuel accompanied him. Years later, he returned to that scene of his filial disobedience, standing bare-headed in the rain in penance. Michael would die a bankrupt in 1731, but the house remained in Johnson's possession until his own death.

Samuel, then, grew up surrounded by books. At the age of seven, he attended Lichfield Grammar School, a precocious child, already from an early age showing the ability to memorise and translate literary works. During his teens, he helped his father in the bookshop,

The Chancel, St. Werburgh's Church,
the setting for the marriage of Samuel Johnson and Elizabeth Porter

ABOVE: *The old key to St. Werburgh's Church*

LEFT: *A carved panel in*
St. Werburgh's Church

The font in St. Werburgh's Church

The Old Grammar School, Ashbourne, where his application as a schoolmaster failed

sometimes employed in stitching the pages of books together, but continuing to study English and classical literature.

In 1728, he went up to Pembroke College, Oxford, but had to leave after only a short time, due to lack of money. The next few years, when he was in his late teens and early twenties, would be years of struggle. He was ambitious, and had dreams of becoming a schoolmaster. There was an unsuccessful application for a post at Ashbourne Grammar School. In 1732, he was employed as an under schoolmaster at Market Bosworth Grammar School, the only teaching post open to a man without a degree. His scholarship, however, continued to deepen, and in the same year, he brought out his first book, an English translation of the French, *A Voyage to Abyssinia*.

This then, was the young man who met the Porters in Birmingham in 1732. Even at their first meeting, despite his youth and poverty, Mrs Porter had been impressed. As she told her daughter, "This is the most sensible man that I ever met in my life".

So it was perhaps natural for her to turn to him in her hour of need after she had lost her husband. Certainly, Samuel too appears to have been attracted to her.

So why Derby, rather than Birmingham where Elizabeth lived, or

Samuel's Lichfield?

It seems a quiet wedding was planned. Perhaps the reasons can be found in their backgrounds. Elizabeth was a widow whose husband had died less than a year before. Samuel was still impoverished and was twenty years her junior. She went ahead with the marriage despite objection from her two sons and disapproval by her friends.

The journey to Derby certainly seemed an unpromising start to their married life. They rode separately on horseback, rather than together in a stagecoach. The bride was in tears. On the way, she had hung back and then rode too fast. For Johnson, in his later version of the journey told to Boswell, this was coquettish behaviour. It came, he thought, from reading "too many frivolous old romances"!

So, he decided to be firm, and rode on at his own pace. As the road lay between hedges, she could not become lost, even though he was often out of sight. Eventually, he waited and they arrived at the Church together.

We cannot, of course, think ourselves back, into the attitudes of the eighteenth century, and Samuel was a young man, perhaps determined to assert his authority early in the marriage.

To us today, it seems unfeeling behaviour on what should have been their happiest day. Yet, 'Tetty' to him was his "pretty dear creature". As Boswell wrote, "His regard and fondness for her never ceased, even after her death". On her gravestone in Bromley are the words of Samuel's tribute to his wife, "beautiful, elegant, talented, dutiful", which surely encapsulate his feelings for her. Elizabeth, early in their relationship, remarked on her enjoyment of their conversations. She sacrificed much to marry the poor, unknown young man.

So, it seems to have been a love match on both sides.

And who can reason with love?

We close the door on their wedding, and leave the Church to its shadows and memories.

As we return the key to the Museum across the road, we may wander awhile among the paintings by Joseph Wright of Derby, and perhaps pause for coffee and cake in its Café, so as to reflect on the life of Samuel Johnson after his wedding in Derby. It was a journey which would take him to London and fame, to include among his friends, some of the greatest of his day and to be a compassionate benefactor to the poor.

Their married life after that wedding day began auspiciously and

Johnson's early hopes of becoming a schoolmaster were quickly realised, thanks to Tetty's dowry of £600, a substantial fortune in those days. With her capital, they were able to purchase Edial Hall, three miles from Lichfield and so to open a private boarding-school. Unfortunately, though, there were only three pupils! One was destined to become famous as one of the leading actors of his day; his name was David Garrick.

With so few pupils, the school could not flourish. In less than a year, it had closed. So, like many a young man before and after him, he set out for London. David Garrick went with him, on his way to school in Rochester. Their journey was a prolonged one, as they only had one horse between them. One man rode for a while, then tied the horse to a tree for his companion to ride the next stage of the journey!

Johnson left for London in March. By October, he had found employment with the publisher, Edward Cave, and was confident enough of his future prosperity to bring Tetty to the capital, to the first of many homes there. Cave published *The Gentleman's Magazine*, and soon Johnson was contributing articles on a wide variety of subjects. His income, though, was insufficient to meet their needs, and perhaps from feelings of guilt at still having to rely on Tetty's money, he removed himself from their home.

In his *Dictionary*, there is an autobiographical hint of his life at this time, when he was living as a bachelor, often sleeping rough or in taverns, or roaming the streets with fellow-writer, Richard Savage. The word 'Grub street' he defines as originally referring to a street "much inhabited by writers of small histories, dictionaries and temporary poems, whence any mean production is called grub street" – a wry reference to his precarious life in the alleys off the real Grub Street, close to Moorfields.

But, he continued to write. He had begun a play called *Irene* while still at Edial, which he now completed. In 1738, his first major work, a satirical poem entitled *London*, was published. Articles poured from him. His friendship with the poet Savage, who died as a debtor in prison resulted in a compassionate psychological biography, *The Life of Richard Savage*.

Gradually, his special abilities were noticed, and in 1746, a group of publishers commissioned him to compile a *Dictionary of the English Language*. Here at last was not only recognition, but a regular income. He and Tetty moved to a house at Number 17, Gough Square, just off Fleet Street, where he employed six assistants and devoted the attics to the necessary space and arrangements used to produce such a monumental work. The house can still be visited, and is now owned by a Trust.

The *Dictionary* was published in 1755, to widespread acclaim. To this day, Doctor Johnson is remembered for this great literary achievement, and is often called 'Dictionary Johnson'. That same year, he was awarded a Master of Arts degree by Oxford University.

In the early fifties, he wrote two hundred essays on moral and religious topics for *The Rambler*. Sadly, however, success and fame continued to be marred by personal tragedy. Tetty had suffered from ill health over the years, and had increasingly turned to alcohol and opiate medicine. In 1752, she moved into the countryside, to rented lodgings, where she died. Mrs Johnson was buried in Bromley, Kent.

Financial problems dogged him too. The salary for his work on the dictionary had finished with its publication. So, he still relied on his other writings for his income. The essays for *The Rambler* were followed by a weekly series, *The Idler*, a philosophical novel, *Rasselas*, and an annotated edition of Shakespeare's plays. Even so, he was twice arrested for debt.

By now, however, Johnson had become what would nowadays be called a 'national treasure'. He was well-known, even among the highest circles in the land. In 1762, a government pension was awarded him. He would never be wealthy, but the pension met his daily needs. Further honours were heaped upon him – an honorary doctorate from Trinity College Dublin in 1765, and another ten years later from Oxford University. He was now 'Doctor Johnson', famed for his writings, but also for his wise and witty conversation. A worthy stage for the great man's eloquence was provided, in 1763, by the formation of The Literary Club, which met in Gerrard Street, Soho, and whose members included Garrick and Reynolds.

In that year, too, he met James Boswell, a meeting which led to their friendship and to Boswell's *Life of Samuel Johnson*. The two men set off on an adventurous tour of the Hebrides in 1773, less than thirty years after Bonnie Prince Charlie's Rebellion. On the island of Skye, there would be a fascinating meeting with the Prince's brave saviour, Flora MacDonald. Johnson was impressed by the heroine. It would be his words, "a name that will be mentioned in history, and if courage and fidelity be virtues, mentioned with honour" – which would be inscribed on her tombstone. The tour led to the writing of two books by the intrepid authors.

For the last twenty years of his life, Doctor Johnson was the leader of the London literary world, a media celebrity of the eighteenth century.

Peter Martin, in his biography, describes him as, "the voice of the age, the rationalist epitome and sage of the Enlightenment".

For Pat Rogers, in the *Oxford Dictionary of National Biography*, he was "Outside Shakespeare, perhaps no-one in English history has become such a representative figure of his age, and no-one has done more to dignify the literary profession in Britain".

Yet the tension between fame and ill-fortune remained for the rest of his life. The perennial health problems were increased by the addition of others such as gout. There were still the moods of depression, the bouts of loneliness, and the intense longing for company. But surely, these, too, were symptomatic of his greatness, his stature as a human being, that he could overcome so many problems and achieve so much.

It is indeed fitting that his final resting place should be among kings and princes, in Westminster Abbey.

TO ASHBOURNE

So, let us now take up his story at the door of Saint Werburgh's Church in Derby.

The years passed after his wedding in the city, but Samuel Johnson's connections with Derbyshire remained. Ashbourne especially for him would be a town of many memories – of disappointments and of convivial visits to his old school friend Dr John Taylor.

In 1732, before his marriage, and still a young man, he had un-successfully applied to be a teacher at the Grammar School. Perhaps it is as well that he was rejected, for had he been accepted, his life and English literature would no doubt have been very different.

Samuel Johnson in later years
From an engraving after Sir Joshua Reynolds

But Doctor Johnson would know happiness too in the old market town. For here lived Dr. John Taylor, the wealthy, so-called 'King of

*Hand coloured engraving of 'Ashbourne Hall, the Seat of Sir
William Boothby' c1850*
Published by Dawson and Hobson, Ashbourne.

Dr. John Taylor's house, Ashbourne

16

Sign above the door to Dr. John Taylor's house, Ashbourne

Ashbourne'. From 1740–1784, Johnson was a regular visitor to his friend's comfortable home. One journey, made from Lichfield in 1776 with Boswell, was in "Dr. Taylor's large, roomy post-chaise, drawn by four stout, plump horses, and driven by two steady, jolly postilions".That was the way to arrive in Ashbourne! It was an unusual friendship, for they seemed to have little in common. Taylor was a clergyman certainly, but was much more interested in his farming ventures and livestock! "Sir, I love him," Johnson told Boswell, "but I do not love him more; my regard for him does not increase. His talk is of bullocks". It is reported too, that his guest wrote twenty five sermons for Doctor Taylor. But the charms of an understanding friend – and it was a lifelong friendship – were strong enough to draw him back often to Ashbourne. He appears to have delighted in hay-making, talking in the garden, writing with his friend in the classical summerhouse, the occasional musical evenings and the quieter life of a country town. It doubtless became increasingly appealing during those busy years in London. In the neighbourhood too were many families whose company and conversation he enjoyed. His room was always the same one. The only disappointment came during his last visit, when Taylor was refurbishing the house. As Johnson said, he was among "ruins and rubbish". He soon moved on!

The attractions of Ashbourne drew Samuel Johnson there very often – reason enough for us too, to follow him.

How would he have appeared had we seen him walking towards us, a tall, lean man, dressed in the grey curled wig, tri-corn hat, long coat and high boots of his time? First impressions would be disconcerting, as they were for his biographer James Boswell when they met by chance in Davies' Bookshop, Covent Garden in 1763. Boswell described him as, "Very slovenly in his dress and speaks with a most uncouth voice". But he was so captivated by Johnson's personality that they soon became firm friends, a friendship which would last over the years. For Boswell added, "Yet his great knowledge and strength of expression command vast respect and render him excellent company".

Seven years after that meeting in Covent Garden, Sir Joshua Reynolds painted Johnson's portrait. It shows him in grey wig and brown coat, painted with an earnest expression across a heavily-jowled face, as though engaged in deep thought. Johnson's friend Sir John Hawkins thought it a good likeness, as it showed "that appearance of a labouring, working mind, of an indolent reposing body, which he had to a very great degree".

However, although Johnson appeared robust, childhood illnesses had affected his strength and appearance. Scrofula and small pox had damaged his sight and hearing, and his face too bore the scars of the diseases. Many portraits show him peering, one holding the manuscript he is reading near to his eyes. He suffered from what is now known as Tourette's Syndrome. Odd gestures, nervous tics and gesticulations would manifest themselves when he was thinking and speaking, his head tilted to the right. The black dog of depression haunted him over the years, and as an antidote, he sought company. "Sir", he once said,"I am obliged to any man that visits me".

Against this dark background of poverty and disability, his achievements shine out more strongly. His life was one of courageous battling against adversity and physical weakness. He was, too, a compassionate, generous man, who supported impoverished friends in his own home even when he himself was poor. His humane nature is reflected in the care he showed towards his Jamaican servant Frank Barber, whom he educated and treated like a son, making him the main beneficiary of his estate. In later years, he employed Anna Williams as his housekeeper, even though she was blind. A devout Anglican, he would be a regular worshipper at St. Oswald's. His constant struggle against the many problems he encountered from childhood onwards, make him a remarkable man, even without his literary achievements. He well-deserves the description as one of the greatest of all Englishmen, a towering intellect, witty conversationalist and wise moral philosopher.

So, let us walk the streets of Ashbourne, in the footsteps of the great man. The 109 or 'Swift' buses take one from Derby to the town, set in a bowl of gentle hills, with the heights of Dovedale as a backdrop. From Ashbourne bus station, we walk over the bridge across Henmore Brook, and soon come to a T-junction. There is a temptation to turn right into St. John's Street. We could easily pass under the gallows sign of the 'Green Man' coaching inn which spans the street. From there, it is but a few steps to the sloping market square with its surrounding shops and cafés.

But resist – for to turn left into Church street is to walk straight in to a film set for *Middlemarch* or *Persuasion*. Wide stone-slabbed pavements carry one past buildings which Doctor Johnson would have known. One can almost imagine him coming towards one, engaged in animated conversation. Here is the Elizabethan Grammar School, once the scene of his unsuccessful interview. Ahead is the spire of Saint Oswald's Church, where he often worshipped.

The interior of St. Oswald's Church, Ashbourne

19

St. Oswald's Church, Ashbourne

LEI·CHE·L·CIEL·NE·MOSTRA·TERRA·N'ASCONDE·

LE·CRESPE·CHIOME·D'OR·PVRO·LVCENTE·
E·L·LAMPEGGIAR·DELL·ANGELICO·RISO·
CHE·SOLEAN·FAR·IN·TERRA·VN·PARADISO·
POCA·POLVERE·SON·CHE·NVLLA·SENTE·

ABOVE: *The tomb of Penelope Boothby in St Oswald's Church, Ashbourne*

LEFT: *A carved head in St Oswald's Church, Ashbourne*

The Church dates from the early thirteenth century. Among its treasures are a Pre-Raphaelite style window by Christopher Whall, and the white marble tomb of young Penelope Boothby. The statue on the top shows her peacefully asleep, dressed in a simple flowing gown with a wide sash. But the inscription beneath gives an added poignancy. For Penelope was the only daughter of Sir Brooke and Lady Susannah Boothby, and died at the age of six. Her parents' marriage seems to have been already at breaking point. Her death was the final calamity – they parted at her grave. As the sad inscription says, "She was in form and intellect most exquisite. The unfortunate Parents ventured their all on this frail Bark. And the wreck was total."

But, let us return to the daylight and the present, for it is the setting of the Church, especially in the Springtime when it seems to be floating on a lake of daffodils, that surely must be its greatest beauty.

Old almshouses and elegant brick three-storey houses line the street. And on the left, just before the Church, is 'The Mansion House' where Samuel Johnson stayed.

Cross over the road first, and one has some idea of its grandeur. Brick walls surround the grounds, where Johnson once admired the lake and the deer on the lawns. The window to the right above the porch is that of Johnson's bedroom. A walk down School Lane to the right of The Mansion House gives tantalising glimpses of the back of the house. From here, one can see the gables from the seventeenth century and the octagonal room whose chandelier Johnson wished to have lighted (but not on his birthday).

But finally, return to the front, rebuilt by Pickford in 1765. Above the door are faded Latin words. They were written by Doctor Johnson.

"May this house stand until the tortoise walks round the world and until the ant drains the ocean waves".

How he must have loved his visits here! Let us, too, not hurry away.

*The Drawing Room of The Mansion House, Ashbourne
(architect Robert Adam 1761-63), by H. Hinge 1932*
By kind permission of Derby Local Studies Library

23

Woodcut of Jane Austen, used in the 1870 'Memoir' by her nephew
By kind permission of Jane Austen's House Museum, Chawton

2. BAKEWELL – A MATTER FOR PERSUASION?

At the top of the staircase of the Rutland Arms Hotel, Bakewell, is an intriguing notice. It records the tradition that, in 1811, Jane Austen visited Derbyshire, and stayed at the Hotel. Here, so the story goes, she revised her novel, *Pride and Prejudice*, which she had begun to write in 1796. Her stay in the area inspired her to make additions to it. Chatsworth was only three miles away, and became the fitting model for the grandeur of 'Pemberley', the home of her hero Mr Darcy.

In the novel, the heroine Elizabeth Bennet visits Derbyshire with her uncle and aunt, the Gardiners. The holiday, they hope, will help to settle their niece after her mis-guided infatuation with Wickham. So, the party arrive at 'Lambton', a small market town. According to the tradition, this can be identified with Bakewell, with Elizabeth's lodgings being the Rutland Arms Hotel. From the inn, the trio set out for Pemberley, little realising that here Darcy and Elizabeth will meet again, and their love for each other will deepen. The inn itself, then, is the setting for one of the most romantic passages in the book. Elizabeth has received a letter from her sister Jane to say that Wickham has eloped with their younger sister Lydia. Mr Darcy arrives to invite Elizabeth and her relations to dinner shortly after the letter has been delivered. In her distress, she turns to him and confides in him. As the Gardiners and Elizabeth return to her home to comfort the family, the chivalrous Darcy sets off for London to arrange for Lydia's marriage to Wickham. When they meet again after these turbulent events, they can declare their true feelings for each other, and Elizabeth can reveal that it was in Derbyshire that she first really came to know and to love Mr Darcy.

This chapter, then, begins with assumptions. Discussion is for later. Conclusions will be left open until after our own visit is completed.

Let us, then, imagine Jane Austen arriving at Bakewell in 1811. The Miss Austen who alighted from the stagecoach was already thirty-six years old. She was the seventh child and younger daughter of the Reverend George Austen and his wife Cassandra, and was born in Steventon Rectory, Hampshire, in 1775. It would have been a crowded and lively household, for in addition to the Austen children, there were boarders too. Mr Austen tutored several boys, who stayed in the house with the family. Theatricals, reading aloud, games and visits were all enjoyed from her childhood onwards. It must have been a noisy home, full of laughter. Two of Jane's brothers would rise to become admirals, one became a clergyman, another an officer and banker. Her brother Edward was adopted by a wealthy distant cousin Mr Knight, and became his heir. His former bailiff's cottage at Chawton, Hampshire, was to become Jane's final home.

But it was her sister Cassandra who was closest to her. It is thanks to the letters exchanged between them that we know so much of Jane's life and thoughts. The Jane of the letters is a lively, gregarious lady, who delighted in company and parties .

After school in Oxford, Reading and Southampton, her life revolved around her family and their circle of friends. Over the years, her home was always with her parents and sister, at first in Steventon, later in Bath and Southampton, and finally in Chawton.

She travelled too. We hear of visits to Devon, Dorset, Wales and Staffordshire, as well as to many parts of Hampshire.

There was, though, much more to Jane Austen than the girl who delighted in balls and the society of others. From her earliest years, she was writing – stories, letters and novels. By her twenties, she had written 'Elinor and Marianne', to be known as *Sense and Sensibility*, an earlier version of *Pride and Prejudice* called 'First Impressions', and *Northanger Abbey*. In 1811, the 'Bakewell' year, she was working on *Mansfield Park*. Later still, there would be *Emma* and *Persuasion*. They would be numbered among the greatest novels in the history of English literature.

So, what of their author? What would Jane have looked like had we seen her in Derbyshire?

Her nephew James-Edward Austen wrote, 'In person, she was very attractive; her figure was tall and slender, her step light and firm, and her whole appearance expressive of health and animation. In complexion she was a clear brunette with a rich colour; she had full red cheeks, with mouth and nose small and well-formed, bright large eyes and brown hair forming natural curls round her face.'

Others, too, who knew her, praised her colourful complexion, large eyes, and quick step. People crowd her letters, and she obviously enjoyed their company and observing their behaviour. Her 'humour' and 'animation' were mentioned by Tom Fowle, a friend from childhood. Perhaps Jane was a little like her favourite heroine Elizabeth Bennet!

The famous portrait of Jane, painted by Cassandra, with its close-fitting cap from which her curls still escape, gives the impression of a rather prim-looking lady, with her folded arms and pursed mouth. Certainly, in her later years, she and Cassandra seem to have settled into early middle-age, two spinster aunts to their brothers' children.

But in the descriptions of her contemporaries, Jane sparkles!

Was there, then, any 'Mr Darcy' in her own life? There was one known proposal, which happened in 1802. Jane was staying with old friends, the Biggs sisters and their father at Manydown House, Hampshire. Their younger brother Harris was there too – a shy young man five years younger than Jane, and heir to the house and estate. When he proposed one evening, she accepted. By the next morning, she realised she had made a mistake, and tactfully explained that she could not marry him. She liked him as a friend, but did not love him.

Her sister Cassandra, years later, recalled another young man whom Jane met about that time. Jane and her parents were staying at a seaside resort in Devon. There they met a 'charming young man', with whom Jane became friendly. The unknown man expressed a wish to meet her again, but sadly died before the next Summer.

The meeting, though, with perhaps the real love of her life, happened when she was twenty. She had been invited to a Christmas ball at Manydown House, where later Harris Biggs would propose. Among the young men was Tom Lefroy from Ireland, who was staying nearby with his uncle and aunt, friends of the Austens. He was handsome and clever, already with a degree from Dublin University. In time, he would become Lord Chief Justice of Ireland. Now he was about to study for the Bar in London. He and Jane met at three balls. They enjoyed dancing and chatting together – and from Jane's letters to Cassandra, flirting too! But it was all over very quickly. He had his studies to complete and a career before him. Neither was wealthy. It seems that if he did return to Hampshire, his aunt kept him well away from Miss Austen. Eventually he married and had seven children.

Did he still remember Jane? It seems that he did. When he was an old man, he mentioned to his nephew that he had been in love with her, 'though it was a boyish love'.

But, what of Jane herself? From her letters, it sounds as though it was a flirtation between two young people who were strongly attracted to each other. Was it, perhaps, though something deeper for Jane, which she would not wish to acknowledge, even to those closest to her, – a first and only love? The writer of novels such as *Persuasion* seems to have known the pain and joy of falling in love – they certainly appear to have been written from personal experience.

And, shortly after that Christmas, she began to write the love story of Mr Darcy and Elizabeth – *Pride and Prejudice*.

Let us now, then, travel to the 'Lambton' of today, – by car or the Transpeak or 6.1 buses from Derby, rather than by stagecoach or carriage!

Beyond the town, meadows level out into the valley. But to the North lie the limestone walls and uplands of the White Peak, – a wilder landscape, where the layer of civilisation is thinly stretched over the ancient hills.

Bakewell itself nestles in a bowl of wooded hills through which the River Wye wanders. A much-photographed fourteenth century bridge crosses the river, beside whose banks is an attractive promenade. It is a delightful place in which to while away part of an afternoon. An ice-cream van is often parked nearby, and one can sit and watch the geese and ducks, and the glittering waters of the Wye as they race across the weir. One could easily imagine oneself at a seaside resort, but without the crowds. In Autumn, the gold and bronze trees paint stunning reflections in the river. Springtime brings fresh greens and yellows to mist the woods on the far side of the valley. Even in Winter, perhaps especially so, there is a beauty to this stretch of the Wye. A frosty stroll in the riverside park, followed by hot chocolate in a cafe a few minutes away, is always enjoyable. There are many from which to choose, but one of the most delightful is 'Byways', upstairs in Water Lane. It's still a 'teashop as teashops used to be', with coal fires in the Winter and a warm welcome!

The houses of Bakewell are like the gold sediment settled in a prospector's pan. They are built of warm stone which looks sunlit even on a cloudy day.

But their charms are often hidden. One has to walk up the hillside, down side streets and alleys to find them. Some are in terraces, rows of houses from many ages and in many styles. Rooftops make a pattern against the sky, uneven, gabled, pointed, betraying their different dates of origin. Many, such as Denman House in Bridge Street and the

The bridge over the River Wye, Bakewell

terraces of Castle Street, were built in the eighteenth century. Bagshaw Hall on Bagshaw Hill, Ivy Cottage in Church Street, and the Old Market Hall are a century older. Among the oldest of them all is to be found in Church Lane behind the Church. It was built in the reign of Henry VIII, once called 'Parsonage House', and now the excellent 'Old House Museum' with its fascinating collections of tools and artefacts.

Soaring above them all, and dominating the skyline of the town is the cross-shaped spire of All Saints Church. A short, steep road brings the visitor to the Church – and it well worth the climb! For among its treasures are stones carved over a thousand years ago. They are covered with the rich, intricate criss-crossing lines of the Saxon craftsmen. Some are kept in the porch, others including the pillars of two crosses are in the churchyard. Echoes of the jewellery of the Staffordshire Hoard come into one's mind as one considers the amazing skill of those workers in garnets, gold and Derbyshire stone.

The site of the Church goes back to at least the tenth century. Attached to the Minster Church was a monastery, from whose safe walls priests would have set out to preach the Christian faith. The West front dates from Norman times, and from its ambitious scale, was certainly designed to impress. The builders of later centuries added a thirteenth century chancel; and in the fourteenth century, the porch and beautiful octagonal font. Restoration, inevitably, has continued, but today's Church remains, a living witness to its ancient origins and to the faith of all who have worshipped within its walls.

It seems especially apt, too, that in this 'Lambton' Church is the resting place of Sir George Manners and his wife Dorothy Vernon. For as well as being the setting for the fictional romance of Elizabeth and Darcy, Bakewell is the nearest village to Haddon Hall, the setting for real-life romance. From there, one night, according to family legend, Dorothy eloped with the dashing Sir George. The bridge in its grounds is said to be the one over which the two lovers rode. They married and had four children, who built this splendid Elizabethan monument for their parents.

The beginnings of Bakewell lie in Saxon times – probably as early as the seventh century. First mention of its name comes in the tenth century. It was then called 'Badecan wella' – either 'bath spring' or the wells of a man named Badeca. The settlement was a royal manor, with a large fortification. It must already have been important, as it was chosen to be the meeting-place of Saxon kings. In 920, the rulers of the Scots, Northumbria and Strathclyde came here with their warriors and courts. It is difficult to imagine the pageantry of the arrival of those great kings of long ago in today's village. Yet Bakewell played an important part in the history of Saxon times. For here, a thousand years ago, the rulers came together swore allegiance to Edward the Elder, son of Alfred the Great, as 'Father and Lord'. Perhaps it was the meadow land gently sloping from the Wye on the edge of the town, on the way to Haddon Hall, which once witnessed the colour and sounds of that long-distant royal conference.

Since then, farming, lead mines and mills have all contributed to its story, and to its wealth, seen today in the legacy of its architecture. In 1330, mention is made of its Monday market. This must have already been well-established, since it was described as having taken place 'from time immemorial'. Livestock, butter and grain were bought and

Bakewell Church soars over the town

sold at least as far back as the reign of Edward 111.

The Bakewell of today is still a market town. On a Monday, market day, its streets are thronged. Farmers buy and sell in the new Agricultural Centre across the river. Colourful stalls attract locals and visitors. In the nineteenth century, cattle, pigs and sheep were driven through the streets to different markets.

But in the early years of that century, radical changes were implemented. The Duke of Rutland was 'Lord of the Manor', and he had ambitions to transform and modernise the town. Many old houses were cleared away. The centre was re-planned. At its heart would be The Square.

Overlooking it, in 1803, the former White Horse Inn was demolished and the next year, a new hotel was opened. It was called The Rutland Arms.

Here our visit begins.

It is a solid building, from the outside resembling the country residence of a Georgian gentleman. Glance up at its roof! The large number of chimneys shows the many fireplaces. If one stands across the square, the building looks strong, symmetrical, its appearance no doubt designed to reassure those first travellers. There is a balance to its façade – a balance between the stonework of mottled gold and grey, and the large rectangular windows set in three rows. Framing the entrance is a porch of four white-painted pillars. Above them, and dominating the plainness of the front are the Rutland Arms. These were

31

carved by one of Bakewell's most famous sons – White Watson, botanist, geologist and sculptor.

So, let us climb the stone steps, worn by the footsteps of two centuries, and enter the Hotel. Ahead is the staircase, of plain white supports topped by a brown handrail. Each tread is edged with the carving of a wave. The staircase in its central well forms a tree whose branches take one up to a balcony, then to the landing, and so to the upper two floors. On the ground floor, to the right and left of the stairs, are today's elegant reception rooms, although the remains of earlier divisions can still be seen. Chandeliers shine down on the creams and olive greens of the furnishings, on paintings and the many clocks. The lounge to the left of the entrance contains the original fireplace, of blackened iron with stone hearth in front.

We go up the graceful staircase. First, there is a flight of stairs, then we turn left up more shallow steps, and so to the landing with its large window. From here, we may pause and look out across the Square towards Bath Gardens, the shops and cafés, and so to the wooded ridge of Haddon, hanging above the rooftops.

Beside the door to Room Number Two is a plaque for us to read,

The Rutland Arms, Bakewell

32

and to intrigue us. For it was in this room, according to hotel tradition, that Jane Austen stayed, and revised 'First Impressions', adding local colour, and revising it, to become *Pride and Prejudice.*

So, let us go back in our imagination to 1811. The roar of the modern traffic fades away. Instead, we hear horses' hooves and the swish of carriage wheels. Coaches arrive and drop their passengers at the entrance before turning across the road. On the opposite side of the Square are the magnificent stables, with two courtyards divided by a great arch. From inside the Hotel, the light of many candles shines out into the streets. We thankfully enter the warmth of the thick stone walls. A fire burns in the blackened grate. Maids hurry to and fro. One has been called to take us up the staircase to the room on the first floor at the front of the building. A fire has been lit in the room, as it has for each guest. Behind the room is another, one used as a sitting room, the other as bedroom. Everything is new and comfortable, for the Hotel has only been opened for six years. We draw back the curtains and look down into the streets of the small town.

The seventeenth century Bath House with its warm water well and botanical garden is on our left. Some older buildings remain despite the recent replanning. One which catches our eye is called 'The Old Bakewell Pudding Shop', famous today for

The Old Bakewell Pudding Shop

the confection made by accident in this very hotel, when the cook Ann Wheeldon omitted the egg mixture from the pastry and instead poured it over the strawberry jam! Many, though, are new, built at the time of the Hotel, the skyline lower in places than it is today. We gaze towards Haddon woods. There are glimpses still of the water meadows southwards on the road to Matlock. Three miles away lies Chatsworth, already one of the famous 'Wonders of the Peak', and ideal for a carriage ride tomorrow morning.

Do memories, then, of such a stay in Bakewell linger in Jane Austen's mind as she writes of Pemberley?

In Chapter 43, the drive to Mr Darcy's house is described. Elizabeth and the Gardiners enter "a very large park", and drive for some time through woods.

"They gradually ascended for half a mile, and then found themselves at the top of a considerable eminence, where the wood ceased."Ahead was the house, described as "a large, handsome, stone building, standing well on rising ground and backed by a ridge of high woody hills". In front was a stream "of some natural importance" After the party has descended the hill, they crossed a bridge, and so approached the house where Elizabeth would soon meet its owner.

This, then, is Pemberley. It could surely serve too as a description of an arrival at Chatsworth.

Pemberley, moreover, was three miles away from Lambton, as is Chatsworth from Bakewell. There are perhaps echoes of its hotel in the inn at Lambton. For Elizabeth could look down into the street to see a carriage approaching the lodgings, just as today one may look down towards Matlock Street from Room 2. Both are upstairs rooms – for Mr Bingley's quick step could be heard as he ascended the staircase. Then again, in chapter 43, the name 'Bakewell' is dropped tantalizingly in Elizabeth's conversation with Darcy, as she explained "indeed, before we left Bakewell, we understood that you were not immediately expected in the country." Where was she when she learned this piece of information, but in 'Lambton'? The two places seem to have become interchangeable in the writer's mind.

1811 is the year traditionally held to be that of Jane Austen's visit. She was already living in her final home – Chawton in Hampshire. If she did visit Derbyshire from there, one would expect to find some reference to it in her letters. These exist from the first part of 1811, until June that year, but there are no plans for a tour mentioned in them. There are then no surviving letters until October 1812. So it must be an argument from silence.

The other possible date is 1806. In this year, she had travelled as far north as Staffordshire, so a journey, which would take two days, into Derbyshire would be practicable. From October that year, she was ill with whooping cough, so it would need to have been made in an earlier month.

There was also certainly information available to her about Derbyshire, without the necessity of a visit to confirm the facts. Many books had already been published by this time describing stately homes and their grounds. Several of these mansions could well have been the model for 'Pemberley'. Indeed, Jane's brother Henry remembered her fascination as a child with Gilpin's *Observations Relative Chiefly to Picturesque Beauty*. Chatsworth was one of the places described in the book.

Perhaps, too, a member of Jane's family, or one of her friends, had visited Derbyshire, and told her of its celebrated 'Wonders'.

Did she perhaps travel there in her imagination? A remote region with a palatial residence in its heart would be an ideal setting for the home of her Byronic hero Darcy. It was distant enough to be romantic and intriguing. Derbyshire was by then, a region famed for its wild beauty. The visitor was drawn there partly because of its situation, to travel to which would be seen as quite an adventure. Pemberley's park is extolled because it has a natural beauty. Elizabeth had "never seen a place for which nature had done more'" This is the idealised landscape of an eighteenth century estate, where trees, hills and water combined to form a harmony. Chatsworth then, at this time would certainly encapsulate this romantic vision of tamed nature, as seen from William Marlow's painting of the house. Both the reality and the fictional are in agreement in this. So perhaps the 'Palace of the Peak', which she had read about and seen in pictures, provided the perfect house and estate for her hero. The charms of Derbyshire will always weave their magic, whether the visit is made in imagination through the pages of a book, or in real life.

So, the visitor of today can ask questions, and discuss; and perhaps dream a little too of one of England's best-loved writers, and of her delightful heroine Lizzy Bennet and romantic hero Fitzwilliam Darcy!

Portrait of Erasmus Darwin by Joseph Wright c1792-3

3. Breadsall, and the Elusive Doctor Darwin

For so large a man – he was six foot tall and heavily built – Erasmus Darwin is surprisingly elusive in Derbyshire!

Visitors to Lichfield will see an imposing brick house in the Cathedral Close. It is worth straying across the border into Staffordshire to visit it. The house looks onto the Cathedral, and has a delightful herb garden. Inside, there is a fascinating museum devoted to the life of the eminent doctor and writer.

In Derbyshire, the places connected with him are there, but not always apparent. They are to be found, though, and will repay the search and the discovery.

Some remain, and are open to the public. The village of Breadsall certainly falls into this category. Others, we can only learn about from records and old pictures.

So, before we set off on an architectural trail, it is perhaps helpful first to pause and gather some information about the man himself and his life.

INTRODUCING DR. DARWIN

Erasmus Darwin was born in 1731 in Nottinghamshire, in the village of Elston, five miles south of Newark He was the son of a barrister. After reading medicine at St. John's College, Cambridge, he completed his studies at the Edinburgh Medical School. The young doctor spent a few unhappy months in Nottingham, but in 1756, moved to Lichfield. In December 1757, he married Mary Howard, a local solicitor's daughter and acquired the attractive house in the Close. Theirs was a very happy marriage.

Throughout the 1760s, they and their three sons – Charles, Erasmus junior, and Robert continued to live in Lichfield. But from there, Dr. Darwin travelled widely in the Midlands and soon built up a reputation as a trusted and eminent physician. In fact, he would be recommended to the King himself, George 111. Darwin, though, resisted the lure, and remained firmly attached to the Midlands. He designed his own carriage, complete with special compartments for food and books. In later years, his horse, 'Doctor', was tethered to it, saddled and ready to ride in case the roads became impassible for the carriage. The state of the roads was such that Darwin turned his inventive skills to the design of a springs and steering system, still in use to this day.

The happy life in Lichfield was sadly not to last. His wife Mary died in 1770, aged only thirty. Darwin as a busy doctor, needed someone to help him in the running of his house and the upbringing of his sons, one of whom was Robert, the father of the naturalist Charles Darwin. At first, his sister Susannah came to support the family. She was soon joined by Mary Parker, perhaps originally from Elston, who entered the household as Robert's governess. Erasmus and Mary fell in love. Between 1772 and 1774, she bore him two illegitimate daughters, Susan and Mary Parker. Darwin acknowledged paternity, and later set them up as schoolteachers in Ashbourne. He even wrote a prospectus for them, its views on female education, years ahead of its time.

Perhaps he eventually would have married Mary Parker. But fate, in the form of the artist Joseph Wright, took a hand. Wright was engaged in various paintings for Radburn (now Radbourne) Hall near Derby. It was the home of Colonel Pole and his wife Elizabeth. In 1771, when Wright was commissioned to paint their portraits, Colonel Sacheverel Pole needed the advice of a doctor. The artist had no hesitation in recommending his friend Erasmus Darwin. Then in 1775, Darwin was invited to treat the three Pole children. Frequent journeys from Lichfield to Radbourne would be made to tend the children – and in time, no doubt in the hope of seeing their mother. In 1778, when the children were ill, she came to stay in his Lichfield house for a few weeks. Erasmus had fallen heavily in love with Elizabeth. Over the next six years, although she was married, more than twenty passionate poems to her would pour from him. They had a shared love of gardens. Indeed, one of his early poems in her praise follows her advice not to prune his trees. Later, Darwin purchased land a mile from Lichfield to transform into a botanic garden.

Then in 1780, Colonel Pole died, leaving a 33 year-old wealthy and beautiful widow. Next year, Erasmus, now 50, and Elizabeth were married in Lichfield. Their marriage would be a long and contented one, and produce seven children.

At the start of their married life, Elizabeth refused to leave

Radbourne. But Darwin's travels as a doctor were wide, and a more convenient place to live had to be found. So they came to Derby, and to a large terraced house at Number Three, Full Street, with gardens down to the Derwent. There, Darwin continued to work as a doctor. When in 1793, his son Robert suggested retirement, his reply was. 'It is a dangerous experiment, and generally ends either in drunkenness or hypochondriacism!'

By 1801, however, he had developed health problems and wished to find a quieter place in which to live. His son Erasmus junior had bought Breadsall Priory in 1799. But within a month, he was found drowned in the Derwent, either as the result of an accident or as suicide. As he was unmarried, Breadsall Priory was left to his father. Darwin was heart-broken at his son's death, and asked to be buried next to him in Breadsall Church.

On March 25th 1802, the Darwin family moved to the Priory. Darwin was already ill, and died a few weeks later, on April 18th. He was buried in All Saints Church, Breadsall.

Such then, are the main facts of his life.

What is known of his appearance? The portraits by his friend Joseph Wright of Derby show him to be a rosy-cheeked man, his jacket straining across a portly frame. He had a sweet tooth and enjoyed his food, although he was largely abstinent from wine. Wright has rather 'tidied' him, for we know that his wig was often at an angle and he was negligent over his clothes. One portrait when he was sixty, shows him with quill poised, as though in deep thought, gazing into the middle distance before he begins to write. In another, painted when he was thirty eight, the doctor leans forward, with a direct look, as though to listen to us and give us his opinions. He spoke with wit and clarity, despite having a stutter. Wright's portraits, though, omit Darwin's ready smile, which was often mentioned by those who knew him. His benevolent disposition is apparent in the free medicines distributed to the poor in Derby, and in his humanitarian views, such as those in the campaign for the abolition of slavery. Among his friends he could number the leading intellectuals of his generation – friendships which lasted lifetimes.

To be reckoned as the greatest doctor of his age seems achievement enough for any lifetime. But Erasmus Darwin was far more than that. He was a many-faceted man, whose interests and talents led him to pioneering contributions to many fields. Truly a 'Renaissance man', his active mind would invent, examine and research, and express itself equally well in poetry or prose.

Darwin was one of the founder members of the 'Lunar Society of Birmingham'. This group of inventors and thinkers met monthly to dine and discuss. They gathered on the night of the full moon, so that they could travel more safely – hence the name 'Lunar'. The members were the gifted men of the Enlightenment, philosophers, chemists, engineers and mathematicians. Among them were the engineer James Watt, the industrialist Matthew Boulton, Joseph Priestley the chemist, and the clockmaker and geologist John Whitehurst. Others later included the potter Josiah Wedgwood, Sir Joseph Banks the botanist, and the American politician Benjamin Franklin as a corresponding member. After Darwin's move from Lichfield, the Derby Philosophical Society would continue to provide a forum for the exchange of ideas and creativity – meeting at the King's Head Inn in the Cornmarket.

Erasmus was a prolific writer and often used poetry as the vehicle for his ideas. His major works include *The Botanic Garden*, 'Zoonomia' or *The Laws of Organic Life*, *The Philosophy of Agriculture and Gardening*, and *The Temple of Nature*.

After the publication of *The Botanic Garden*, many of his contemporaries considered him to be the greatest English poet of their age. Romantic poets such as Wordsworth and Shelley were much influenced by his pastoral style. Indeed, Coleridge called him the 'first literary character in England'.

But the poems reflect, too, his encyclopaedic knowledge and the inventiveness of his mind. Subjects ranged from the classification of plants, the study of diseases and their cures, and the science of gardening. He inserts, almost as passing references, his conclusions about the formation of the moon, the components of water, 18th century industries, and foretells steam-powered vehicles, even ones that could fly!

It is, though, in *The Temple of Nature* that we see him at his most revolutionary. For him, life had begun in the sea, in microscopic forms. These developed into the higher plants and animals, until 'imperious man' appears. Erasmus has long been called the 'grandfather of Charles Darwin'. But his own genius had led him to explore the concept of evolution long before *The Origin of Species*.

Darwin was an inventor too, although he never patented his ideas, as he was concerned for his reputation as a doctor. A copying machine, an artesian well, a model flying bird, speaking machine, horizontal windmill, ventilation devices, and a canal lift for barges are just a few of so many inventions to emerge from his brilliant mind!

This, then, was the man at the heart of the Enlightenment, in Lichfield and later in Derby.

But are there any buildings which survive from his life?

IN DERBY

A good place to begin our rambles is in the Market Place in Derby. Between the Tourist Information Office and the Assembly Rooms, (built, alas! as a dire example of 60s concrete architecture) is an opening which takes one into Full Street. Ahead is Exeter Bridge spanning the Derwent. To one's right is the Council House, refurbished inside but with its original facade; and the listed Magistrates Court, now the excellent Local Studies Library. It is well worth a visit, both for its elegant entrance and staircase, as well as for its 'courtroom' centre. Immediately to the left of the Library soars the modern Jury's Inn, built on the site of the former Police Station. The Library and Hotel stand on the site of the gardens of Darwin's house. Beyond these, there is a pleasant, open view of the river and of the old Silk Mill, now one of Derby's Museums. If there is time, one can take the path along the River Derwent to the village of Darley Abbey, about a mile away. It makes for a delightfully peaceful walk, with the reward of tea and cakes at the Café in Darley Park as its conclusion.

We have to picture, though, a very different scene in our imagination if we visited this part of Derby at the time of Dr. Darwin. In the eighteenth century, Full Street would be lined with attractive town houses of differing styles. A mansion called Exeter House, where Bonnie Prince Charlie made his fateful decision to turn back to Scotland rather than to continue to London, once stood on the site of the Magistrates Court. It was demolished in 1834, although some of its panelling is now in Derby Museum. A statue of the Prince in highland dress, gazing wistfully towards the South, now stands on Cathedral Green. Adjacent to Exeter House, at Number Three, there stood an imposing three-storey brick and stone house with large windows which once was home to the Darwins. It was built in 1722 and demolished in 1933. Years later, after the family's move to Breadsall, it became the town house of the Curzons of Breedon, and later the local

41

Derby, Local Studies Library, Full Street, on the site of the gardens of Darwin's house

Full Street Derby pencil and watercolour by Peter Perez Burdett 1769
© 2017 Derby Museums Trust

Photograph of Full Street, 1930s
By kind permission of Derby Local Studies Library.

Conservative Club.

In the Darwins' day, it must have been a delightful home. Gardens sloped down to the Derwent, and the doctor built a riverside pavilion. He had land, too, on the opposite side of the river, planted as an orchard. A self-operated rope ferry was installed by him, and an artesian well was sunk in the grounds to provide fresh water.

Around the corner in Queen Street lived the artist Joseph Wright and the scientist and clockmaker John Whitehurst. The cartographer Peter Perez Burdett's home was a Gothic-style house in Full Street.

Traces of the elegance of the interior of the Darwin house survive in a sketch by Erasmus' granddaughter. It shows Erasmus emerging from his study, as his children play on a sweeping staircase. On the wall is a clock, no doubt by Whitehurst. In a silhouette of the 1790s, Darwin and his son are seated at a table, playing chess; and in Derby Museum, the wrought iron fanlight, designed by Bakewell, survives. What a delightful town Derby must have been for them to live in, with such neighbours, so many attractive houses, and All Saints' Church, now the Cathedral, along the road!

Sadly, no signs of the house itself remain in the busy city centre. Only a blue plaque on the wall of the Assembly Rooms as one emerges into Full Street, reminds the passer by that Dr Darwin once lived across the road.

TO BREADSALL

If we journey,though, four miles northwards along the Derwent, we come to Breadsall. It is a small village, and seems especially peaceful after leaving the nearby A38 and Abbey Hill Roundabout. The Number 59 bus from Derby to Ilkeston takes us there. Attractive residences line its few streets. On the rise of land stands the Church, screened by trees. Across the road is the Old Hall, an intriguing building, once the manor house, dating back to at least the fifteenth century, but with much alteration in the nineteenth century.

We may wish to pause for lunch at the nearby Garden Centre. But, then, we will leave the village and travel along the old Roman Rykneld Street to Breadsall Priory. For we will visit the Church at the end of our time in Breadsall.

AT THE PRIORY

The Priory was Darwin's final home. After the tragic death of his son in 1799, Erasmus inherited the house. He had at last decided to retire.

Erasmus' son had been full of plans for alterations to his home when he bought it in 1799. But there was still much to be done before the family could settle there. A three-bay extension and much 'modernisation' were completed, and in 1802, the Darwins moved in. Darwin loved the house and its setting. He described it as 'a pleasant house, a good garden, ponds full of fish, and a pleasing valley – deep, umbrageous, and with a talkative stream running down it.'

Today, then, as we leave Breadsall village and the Derwent Valley behind us, the road climbs steadily. It is known as 'Moor Road', and so we might expect a wilder landscape. But it is tamed and cultivated, and surprisingly gentle, rather different from that suggested by its name. If we pause and look back, we see the hills on the other, western, side of the River. Allestree unfolds along the horizon, its skyline broken by poplars. The water tower at the back of Allestree Park is visible for a moment, and the soaring glassy walls of Derby University too. In Darwin's day, the Cathedral tower, four miles away, could be seen from his house. But trees must have obscured that view from 200 years ago.

Very soon – sooner perhaps than we would expect – we see vivid slanting lawns on the left side of the road. They roll softly down a sheltered valley, lined and pierced by groups of trees. Where once the Priory brothers walked and worked, golfers now pace the emerald grass, like slow-moving dancers from a distant masque.

There, towards the upper slope of the valley nestles the Priory. It is as perfect a setting for a house as one could wish. No wonder Darwin praised its beauty! The hills and trees enfold it, – an enchanting combination of shades of green surrounding walls of warm pink-grey local stone.

Breadsall Priory nowadays is a hotel, the oldest in the Marriott group, and open to non-residents. So, the visitor to Derbyshire is able to enter the Estate. One turns into a drive past the Victorian lodge, and, looking towards the left, one can see the delightful grounds running through the valley. Terraced lawns step down to a fountain pond, one of the original Priory fish-ponds. Paths lead enticingly onwards among the trees towards the Wilderness, where Darwin's favourite horse, Doctor, was buried in 1809.

The Priory is a Russian doll of a house. As we face the East front, we are looking at what appears to be a Victorian residence. The rooms here, with their castellated roofs and large Gothic windows were added in the 1860s. The porch with its turrets leads us to imagine that we are about to enter a castle. This is the world of Sir Walter Scott and

Tennyson, of Highland baronial halls and echoes of a Mediaeval chivalric age. But look higher! For above the porch, at the third storey, there are pointed gables with small windows. These draw us back to Elizabethan times, to the tall E-shaped mansion built by Sir John Bentley (1554 – 1621). It was he who transformed the Priory into a home.

For the Priory of today is a house within a house. The Victorian outer wings are wrapped around an Elizabethan heart, with traces of the Darwin house within its walls. Here and there, if we look carefully, there are even signs of the original Priory.

The earliest building, then, dates from the thirteenth century, and was a house of the Austin Canons. Their name derives from their Rule, attributed to Saint Augustine of Hippo, the great Algerian fourth century Doctor of the Church. They were renowned for their hospitality, and the gardens, orchards and fish-ponds must always have supplied good provisions for the table of the canons and their guests. Breadsall, though, remained a small Priory; it never housed

Breadsall Priory today

46

more than the Prior and two canons at the most. When it was dissolved,in 1536, there was only the Prior who needed to be granted a pension. But although it had small endowments, supplemented by bequests from time to time, it was a place of faith and hospitality. In its Church, too, masses were said for the families who supported it. Like its neighbour in the village below, it was a centre for Christian worship.

Little remains of the 300 years of its religious history. But there are a few glimpses into its past still to be seen today. In the basement, the drains survive from the washing area of the Priory. Fragments of the bake oven are built into the wall near the present day Priory Restaurant on the lower ground floor. There, too, is a fine thirteenth century stone doorway and pointed arches. It seems fitting that guests today dine in a room entered through such a doorway!

On these foundations, then, rose the strong stone walls of Sir John Bentley's mansion. An engraving of 1791 by Ravenhill shows a magnificent gabled hall with farm buildings behind it. On the right is an octagonal dovecote. It is long gone, but would have stood on the

Engraving of Breadsall Priory 1791
published by J Robson, New Bond Street, London

47

incline towards the car park to the right of the entrance. Local families owned the Priory throughout the eighteenth century, but although they made alterations, these have been generally eclipsed by those of the nineteenth century.

However, for a few all too short weeks, Doctor Darwin lived here. Today, as we enter the house, we pause among the Gothic arches and carved pillars of the Victorian age. But if we look ahead, we are gazing into the earlier house. From its sale document of 1859, the Darwin home must have been of a gracious size. It comprised dining and drawing rooms, library, study, 14 bedrooms, kitchen and many rooms for the servants. Outside stood the coach house, stables, and a brew house. At the top of today's stairs, on the left, is a lofty light room. It is shown to visitors as the Library. Perhaps, then, this is an appropriate place in which to reflect on the happiness the Darwin family enjoyed here, as we look from its large bay window across the gardens and hill-sides beyond.

Erasmus' widow Elizabeth continued to live in the Priory until her death in 1832. No doubt among the grandchildren who enjoyed visiting her was Robert's son, Charles. The house then passed to her son Sir Francis Sacheverel Darwin (1786 – 1859). After an adventurous life travelling across Europe and the Middle East, he settled in Breadsall. In his day, wild pigs roamed the woods and tame snakes could be seen in the house, reflecting his antiquarian and natural history studies. He took an active interest in the history of his home, and organised excavations to reveal its past. If you are able to visit the Gun Room, you are actually standing on one of his discoveries – the foundations of the Priory church walls. Another link with the religious story of Breadsall is to be seen in the Reception area. Sir Francis' excavations had also uncovered two beautifully-carved, trefoil-headed arches, possibly sedilia. They help to give us a window into the lost world of the canons and their lovely place of worship.

His daughter Violetta Darwin, too, was interested in architecture – perhaps it is little wonder, growing up in such a house! She became a talented book illustrator, and it is thanks to her that we have so many sketches of the buildings and people connected with her family. From the Priory which she knew, here are two 18th century stone caryatids, perhaps from a chimney piece. We can see these delightful figures as we enter the Priory Restaurant.

A final memory from the Darwins is the dogs cemetery. If we follow the path which skirts the terraced lawns to the right as we walk away from the house, we discover many small headstones. 'Poor Monsieur Dark', inscribed on one, must have been a much-missed pet!

Francis Morley, of the hosiery firm, lived in the house from 1860 – 1883 and was responsible for the Victorian rooms we visit today and which dominate our first views of the house. If one is invited to a wedding reception, it is in one of these that we would dine.

At the end of the nineteenth century, Captain R. R. Rothwell purchased the estate. Among his improvements were the installation of electricity and a supply of pure spring water for the house.

The last family owners were Sir Alfred Haslam, the inventor and manufacturer of fridges and freezers, and his son Eric. A wrought iron Gothic doorway, made for the Great Exhibition in 1851, and now in Reception, as well as fine oak panelling in the Breadsall Room can still be seen. But perhaps the most spectacular legacy of Sir Alfred's life here is the Moorish billiard room, complete with minstrels' gallery.

His son Eric enjoyed his home for forty years and planted many of the trees which we see today. It was in his day that the thirteenth century doorway and drainage system were discovered.

After Eric Haslam's death in 1967, the house remained empty, until the Estate was bought by David Cox in 1971. Major alterations were undertaken to transform it into a Hotel and Golf Course. Whitbread became the owners from 1988; and in 1995, it became part of the Marriott hotel family, remaining so to this day.

A warm welcome still awaits the visitor in the entrance hall. Old furniture, paintings and engravings, may reflect the Priory's long history. But it is, as it always has been, a gracious building with the happy atmosphere of a family home.

RETURN TO THE VILLAGE AND ITS CHURCH

So, after perhaps a coffee or a meal, let us return now to Breadsall village. It is mentioned in the Domesday Book as having a church, priest and mill, and it is the tapering spire of the Church which draws the eye for miles around. A church stood here in Saxon times and was rebuilt in the twelfth century on a large scale. The Norman arch of 1150, with its carved dogtooth work, and the porch both survive, and show something of its splendour. The Church, though, has been restored many times through to the twentieth century.

Then, in 1914, a fire broke out, which devastated the building. It was attributed to the suffragettes, although this is disputed. The fire brigade took an hour to reach Breadsall, and in that hour, a chained library, and all internal woodwork were destroyed. But, phoenix-like, within two years, the Church had been restored and reopened for worship. Today, its warm pink-grey walls defy flame and the passing of time. Before any visit, a key should be first obtained, or opening times checked. Its interior is of great interest. Among the treasures are the large Norman arch and a mediaeval alabaster 'Pieta'. During the Reformation, it had been buried to keep it safe, and then was found in 1877 under the nave, having survived the fire.

It was here in All Saints' Church, on April 24th 1802, that Erasmus Darwin was buried alongside his son. The exact location of his tomb remains unknown, but it was probably in the nave or chancel. No records survive of the burial.

On the wall by the porch, though, is a stone memorial, placed there by his widow.

It reads:

> 'Of the rare union of talents
> which so eminently distinguished him
> as a Physician, a Poet and Philosopher
> His writing remains
> a public and unfailing testimony.

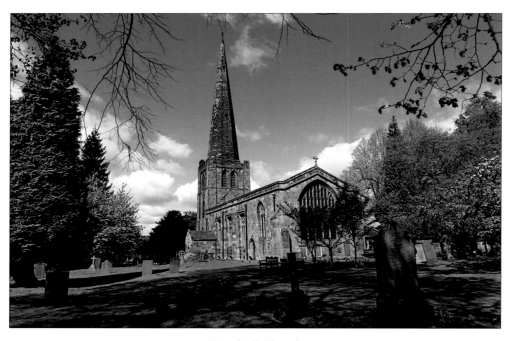

Breadsall Church

Breadsall Church, the chancel

Breadsall Church, the rood screen

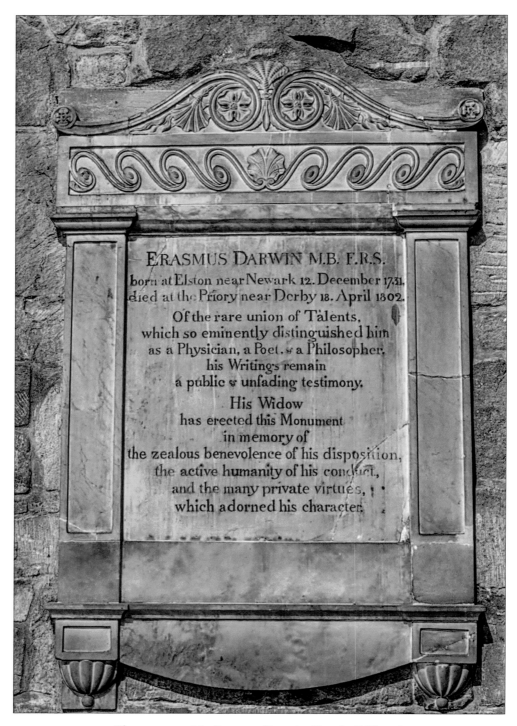

ERASMUS DARWIN M.B. F.R.S.
born at Elston near Newark 12. December 1731.
died at the Priory near Derby 18. April 1802.

Of the rare union of Talents,
which so eminently distinguished him
as a Physician, a Poet, & a Philosopher,
his Writings remain
a public & unfading testimony.

His Widow
has erected this Monument
in memory of
the zealous benevolence of his disposition,
the active humanity of his conduct,
and the many private virtues,
which adorned his character.

The monument to Erasmus Darwin, Breadsall Church

The Norman doorway, Breadsall Church

His widow
has erected this monument in memory of
the zealous benevolence of his disposition
the active humanity of his conduct
and many private virtues
which adorned his character'.

Elizabeth lived in the Priory for another thirty years until her death in 1832. A lively and welcoming lady, she continued to take an active interest in gardening. Her grandchildren enjoyed their visits to her so much that they called the Priory, 'Happiness Hall'.

She was buried in the churchyard of Breadsall Church.

Sir Walter Scott, print by J. Graham,
engraved by T. Woom, c1831 Fisher, Son & Co.

4. Castleton – A Village and its People

It was Sir Arthur Conan Doyle who described the area around Castleton as a "hollow country".

As he wrote in *The Story of the Blue John Gap* from *Tales of Terror and Mystery*, "Could you strike it with some gigantic hammer, it would boom like a drum, or possibly cave in altogether and expose some huge subterranean sea".

Yet, as one walks up the path towards Winnats Pass, and looks back to the village, all seems so solid and reassuring. The Hope Valley in

'View into Hope Dale from Winnats', 1886,
drawn by Sir Francis Chantrey, engraved by G. Cooke

which Castleton nestles, stretches away calmly to the hills. Green fields are ribbed by silver grey walls, some called by the old name 'Flattes', or furlongs, dividing the grassland into long rectangular shapes. Mountains encircle the Valley protectively. All looks stable, timeless. If one could turn the clock back , millennia even, it would appear, one suspects, very similar.

But Arthur Conan Doyle was right.

The information board at the beginning of Winnats, or 'Wing Gates', Pass gives the first clue to a turbulent remote past. Over 300 million years ago, Castleton lay in a shallow lagoon. Creatures swam in its warm waters, their tiny fossil shapes still visible in the surrounding rocks. The steep, sheer sides of the Gates look like cliffs, and infact that is exactly what they are, being the remains of reefs once under water. Volcanic action, storms, Ice Age glaciers and later torrents have all contributed to its story.

Where the Pass defiles between the cliffs, across the road from the

Speedwell Cavern, Castleton

information board, is the entrance to Speedwell Cavern, a former lead mine with an underground stream fed by rain-water through cracks in the rock and miles of natural and man-made tunnels. In the eighteenth century, a canal was dug deep into the earth. Nowadays, one descends to it down

100 steps. There, a boat awaits, to carry one along the dark subterranean stream. At the end is the so-called 'Bottomless Pit', whose great depth is shown by underwater light.

In the hillside to the right of the Pass is the entrance to the Treak Cavern, a cave dripping with stalactites, and from which the subtly-coloured flurospar, called Blue John, is still carefully taken. A mile from Castleton is the Blue John Mine, from whose depths, too, the mineral is extracted.

'View from within Peake Hole near Castleton', 1886, drawn by Sir Francis Chantrey, engraved by G. Cooke

The name 'Blue John' may have been coined by the lead miners to distinguish it from the mineral zinc blende which they called 'black-jack'. Its other origin lies in France ,where many of the early pieces were cut and polished. The French craftsmen called it 'bleu-jaune', as the stone was often blue and yellow. Blue John is only found in the Castleton area and has long been prized for its definite bands of colour. The Roman writer Pliny described valuable vases of banded purple and white, which perhaps were of fluorspar. But the first written reference probably occurs in 1700 when Charles Leigh mentioned the Azure Spar found in copper and lead mines in Derbyshire. It was from the late eighteenth century

The Rope Walk, Peak Cavern, Castleton

onwards that Blue John became highly sought-after for ornamental use. Fluorspar vases, tables, mantelpieces were among the works of art to be found in stately homes such as Chatsworth and Kedleston Hall.

The way to Peak Cavern, Castleton

Later, the spar was used for items of jewellery and small bowls, and these continue to be fashioned by the skilled craftsmen of the village. Mining is by hand as the mineral is brittle. It is then stored for a year to dry out, after which it is sawn, subjected to heat, treated with resin and finally worked. A small piece of jewellery makes a very special memento of a visit to the village.

Behind its houses, too, in a great gash in the cliff, is the entrance to still another cavern. It is called Peak Cavern and is one of the most

58

Mam Tor, Castleton

dramatic cave entrances anywhere in the world. One follows a stream which issues from the cave past a row of cottages towards what seems a solid cliff-face. Above, on the ridge, looms the keep of Peveril Castle, and then, as one approaches the rocky hill, one realises that one is entering a gigantic cave.

A hollow landscape. Millennia of rains have soaked through its surfaces. Streams disappear into the hillsides. To follow them is to enter a dark underground world. Waterfalls drip down its rocks. Stalactite pillars create colonnades. Shadows and shapes conjure mysterious forms to the imagination. The passages continue deeper and lead to tunnels as yet unexplored, far away from the light. One cave, called 'Titan' was only recently discovered and is larger than a cathedral. Who knows how many others are still waiting to be found?

It is an area honeycombed by natural caves, many extended by human skill and efforts. Over the centuries,some have given shelter for human remains have been discovered, along with those of the pre-historic animals – the mammoths and the bears – who once roamed these hills.

Until comparatively recently, people still lived in Peak Cavern. The smoke from their fires blackens its entrance roof to this day, and the modern visitor will see the relics of their mining tools and wooden rope-making apparatus. Descendants of those long-ago villagers often lead the guided tours, and bring their families to life with their tales and humour.

Some sought refuge underground in caves. Others looked to the hilltops for safety and self-defence. Settlements dating from the Bronze Age are to be found on the summits around Castleton. The most massive of these is on towering Mam Tor, its huge earthworks at one time providing protection for hundreds of people. Even without the remains of their huts, MamTor would be

Peveril Castle, Castleton

impressive. The name, 'Shivering Mountain' has been given to it, for its slopes have been shaped by landslides. It is a crumbling, moving mountain, with a cliff-like, pyramid side facing towards Hope Valley

'Mam Tor' can also mean 'Mother Mountain'. The name evidently intrigued Daniel Defoe, who visited the area in 1726. He suggested that, "the soft crumbling earth which falls from the summit produces several other mountains below". Hence the name. It's as good an explanation as any!

Castleton, then, may present a serene face to the modern visitor. But, as has been seen, this is deceptive. Mountains 'shiver'. Hillsides were once beneath the seas. Nature and Man have created caverns and

Cross Street, Castleton

unfathomable underground galleries, and rocks pierce the soil, like the fossil of some sleeping dinosaur,on whose spiny ridge above the town, stands a castle, itself like the jagged bones of some prehistoric monster.
  Built in the eleventh century, in the years shortly after the Conquest,

The George, Castleton

it dominates the valley. The climb to the cube-like keep is well worth the effort, for from here, spectacular views radiate out towards the hills and down Hope Valley. It is no wonder that the powerful Norman lord, William de Peverel, chose this rocky site for his castle. It still bears his name, 'Peveril of the Peak', surely one of the most romantic of titles! From its stout stone walls, the royal High Peak hunting areas and the lead mines could be overseen. For, from 1155, the King owned the High Peak Forest. Henry II visited the castle several times, and in 1157, welcomed King Malcolm IV of Scotland, who came to pay him homage. Towards the end of the fourteenth century, it had come into the possession of John of Gaunt, Duke of Lancaster, who removed some of its masonry for buildings elsewhere and so began its decline. From his time onwards, then, the lands were administered on behalf of the Crown by the Duchy of Lancaster. Today, the castle is in the care of English Heritage, its great curtain walls and imposing keep visible signs of its royal past.

A town grew up at the foot of the castle. In 1192, Richard I gave permission for the building of a new town, its streets laid out in the grid pattern still seen today. At its centre, as so often, was the Church and the market place. Around it were defensive ditches – the remains of which can be seen in the field next to the 'Bull's Head'. Many old houses, including Cruck Houses, line its streets. Among them, one of the most delightful is known as 'Rose Cottage', with its beamed rooms and oasis garden. The Cottage was built on an ancient track way used by people from the village of Edale on their way to the Church. As it was a right of way, one of the doors was kept unlocked until the 1970s, when it was legally closed. Rose Cottage was part of a Cruck Barn, originally used for threshing, and built about 1450. By the late nineteenth century, the barn had been sub-divided into separate properties, and one of these, Rose Cottage, was then used as a tearoom. The traditions of a warm welcome and excellent home-cooked food are still maintained – a perfect blend of an atmospheric old building and contemporary catering for today's hungry visitors.

Castleton is an attractive village, designed for strolling and searching out hidden gems. Some are now cafés and gift shops, where one can buy the world-famous Blue John pieces. But the many inns bear witness to the history of Castleton. Lead- mining was thirsty work!

The town, too, was on the daily route of the Sheffield to Manchester stagecoaches. As far back as 1828, Mrs Margaret Wragg of the Castle

Inn kept post chaises and horses, and offered accommodation to travellers. Tourism was already in evidence!

Lead mining, candle-making, rope-making, cotton weaving and farming have all been part of Castleton's industrial history. But, certainly since the seventeenth century, and no doubt earlier, travellers have visited it – and have been inspired to describe its wonders. There are references to Castleton in Philemon Holland's translation into English of Thomas Camden's *Britannia*, originally written in Latin. Holland, in his book of 1610, included Peak Cavern among his "three wonders" of the Peak, and Peveril Castle in his "three beauties".

The philosopher Thomas Hobbes probably came here from Chatsworth, where he lived for many years. In 1636, he published his book *Seven Wonders of the Peak*. Two were at Castleton – Mam Tor and Peak Cavern.

Charles Cotton, in 1681, compiled a list of the Wonders of the Peak. He too described Mam Tor and Peak Cavern. His complete list is – Poole's Cavern and St. Anne's Well in Buxton, Peak Cavern, Eldon Hole, Mam Tor, Ebbing and Flowing Wells at Tideswell, and Chatsworth.

Daniel Defoe's list is far more limited – and dismissive! In his *Tour through the whole island of Great Britain* of 1726, only Eldon Hole and

Market Square, Castleton

63

Chatsworth are deemed worthy of a mention. The first is as a natural wonder, the second as 'man-made'.

John Ruskin (1819 – 1900), though, must be credited with putting Derbyshire firmly on the tourist map. He described the county as "the most educational of all English landscapes – a lovely children's first alphabet".

Among those tourists was Queen Victoria. In the 1830s, when still a princess, she travelled to Castleton and visited its caverns. She even ventured on to the underground stream, lying flat in the boat like everyone else!

But for sheer courage and real-life drama, the visit of the Reverend Charles Moritz is hard to beat! He was a young idealistic German clergyman, a great admirer of Milton. In 1782, he had come to England with little money, a change of clothing in his pockets, and a copy of Milton's *Paradise Lost*. After staying some weeks in London, he heard of the wonders of Derbyshire. So, on foot, in stagecoaches, usually on his own, he travelled the roads to the Peak.

He arrived in Derby, then a small town, on market day. It was there, as he wrote that, "I began to be always civilly bowed to by the children of the villages through which I passed".

From Derby, he walked to Duffield, Matlock Bath, and Matlock, always noticing the stone houses. At Tideswell, he was impressed by the "very handsome church". And at the welcoming inn, he enjoyed toasted cheese!

Once at Castleton, he wasted no time in searching out the Peak Cavern, the objective of his journey. He described how he followed a stream to its entrance. There he met a local man, who offered to be his guide "for half a crown". Inside the mouth of the great cave was a subterranean village. He recorded the rope-making wheels, and the people enjoying their Sunday rest outside their huts. A lady gave a candle to him and his guide, and so they ventured into the darkness.

He was filled with wonder at the immense cavern. At its limit, they came to a broad stream, where a boat was moored. His guide ordered him to lie flat, and towed the boat to the further shore. A second stream was crossed on the back of his guide! They went on, past stalactites, crawling along low passageways, hearing rain from the cave roof. At last, they faced a wet, slippery slope. His guide helped him to the top, returned for his candle, and then carried him on his back to safety .

At the end of his adventure, his shoes were ruined. But he was told of a friendly shoe-maker, who mended them. The stories Moritz told him of his travels must have made him restless, for he wanted to go with him! After this, Moritz returned to London, and after his two months' stay in England, returned to Germany.

His account is as much about the people he met as of the natural wonders he had seen. The bowing children, the honest guide, the rope-makers, the helpful shoe-maker – they were the people of Castleton.

One of the most illustrious visitors, though, was among the 'celebrities' of his day, famed both in his native Scotland and South of the Border. His name was Sir Walter Scott. Born in 1771, in Old Town, Edinburgh, Scott was the son of a lawyer father, also called Walter, and his wife Anne Rutherford. When Scott was only two or three, he contracted polio, which left him lame in his right leg for the rest of his life. Although he grew up in Edinburgh, his parents sent him to the Borders to help him become stronger. In 1773 and again in 1776, he lived with his grandfather, Robert Scott, on his farm at Sandyknowe in Tweed dale. When his health deteriorated once more, in 1783, he stayed with his aunt Jenny Scott in Kelso. The months spent with his grand-father and aunt were to make a lasting, formative impression on him, for from them, he heard the tales of the heroes and the popular songs of the Borders. He became a strong walker and imbibed the folk lore of the people he met in the countryside. Blessed with an amazing memory, he could both recite the poems and stories he had heard, and write them down, becoming over the years, a recorder of the oral history of the Borders. His delightful store of anecdotes would enter-tain many, from the fellow-students of his youth to the Prince Regent. One unknown traveller who shared a stagecoach journey with him in later years, begged Scott to write down his stories, little knowing to whom he spoke!

Despite, though, the time enjoyed in the Borders, his education was to be in Edinburgh, first at the High School and then at the University. He trained to be a solicitor for five years, so as to become a partner with his father. It was infact on a journey to the Highlands on business for his father that he would meet another great Scottish poet – Robert Burns, the only time they met. In 1792, he qualified as a lawyer and was called to the bar, for the next few busy years, practising as an advocate in Edinburgh. These were years of growing prosperity, punctuated by travels in Scotland, and into the Highlands.

It was at this time, too, that Scott fell in love with Williamina Belsches a baronet's daughter, whom he had first met at Church, sheltering her beneath his umbrella as he escorted her home one rainy day Believing her feelings to be as strong as his, in 1795, he proposed to her. But she had already come to love someone else, and in January 1797, married William Forbes, the son of a wealthy banker. Scott was deeply wounded . Veiled references to his unrequited love for her in his later writings show how the memory lingered over the years, even though he never mentioned her by name again. As he wrote in his *Journal* thirty years later, "Broken-hearted for two years, – my heart handsomely pierced – but the crack remain to my dying day".When a young friend wrote to him in 1813 about his own troubled love affair, Scott would reply, "We build statues of snow and weep when they melt." He had learned to conceal the wound, but the scar would always remain.

His career and travels, though, continued. In 1797, he visited the Lake District. There, he met a vivacious, dark-haired Frenchwoman, Charlotte Carpenter, when she was out riding. Three weeks later, after a whirl-wind courtship, he asked her to marry him. Like him, she had known the sorrow of an unhappy love affair, and they were drawn to each other. On a snowy December day, in Carlisle, they were married. Their life together would prove to be a very happy one, their marriage blessed with four surviving children, and their various homes welcoming places in which to entertain their many friends.

Meanwhile, Scott's success in his legal work prospered. In 1799, he was appointed Sheriff-Deputy, or principal judge, of Selkirk shire, a post he held until his death. By 1806, he had become Principal Clerk to the Court of Session in Edinburgh. He was able to purchase a large, attractive house at 39, Castle Street, a family home until 1826. But the attraction of the countryside remained, and he rented a cottage at Lass wade on the River Esk as a Summer home, and in 1804, a house at Ashestiel near Galashiels. Scott, despite his lameness, was physically strong and vigorous. A skilled horseman, he enlisted in the Light Dragoons and during the threat of Napoleon's invasion, was a volunteer cavalryman.

The distinguished career of a lawyer, however, was only half the picture. That early love of ballads and heroic tales had stayed with him and had developed. Scott was also a man of letters. In the late 1790s, he had translated poetry and dramas from the German. By 1800, he had collected and edited material for a collection of ballads, published in three volumes as *Minstelry of the Scottish Borders*.

Walter Scott, however, rose to overnight fame and adulation when his own poems were published. In 1805, *The Lay of the Last Minstrel*, in

1807 *Marmion* and in 1810 *The Lady of the Lake* followed each other to general popularity and critical acclaim. He had a wonderful way with words. Some of his lines are still with us today.

"But answer came there none". (*The Bridal of Trier main*)

"Breathes there a man, with soul so dead,who never to himself hath said,this is my own, my native land!" (*Marmion*)

"O what a tangled web we weave,
When first we practise to deceive!" (*The Antiquary*)

Novels followed, their titles passing into the library of English classical literature, tales of noble deeds, of chivalry and romance, such as Waverley, Kenilworth, Ivanhoe, Quentin Durward, Rob Roy. *Waverley*, when it appeared in 1814, was the most successful novel ever published in the English language. The works set in prose the poetic tradition in which he had been saturated from his youth. He had the gift of bringing to vital life the people from ages long gone. His heroes and heroines were convincing, with well-observed personalities, even when set against the pageantry of distant, half-forgotten times. The settings too, especially those in his native Scotland, were so romantic and vivid, that they drew visitors to the Highlands. Walter Scott can be said to be the founder of the genre of the historical novel.

The financial prosperity resulting from his poetry enabled Scott to purchase, in 1811, Cartley Hole Farm near Mel rose. The house was extended and remodelled in 'baronial' style, becoming famous as 'Abbotsford'. To his stately hall, he brought his books, but also weapons and furniture, even stonework, from historic places in Scotland. It was a fitting home for the 'Laird of Abbotsford'.

For by 1814, Scott was renowned as the 'Wizard of the North', a man who was fêted in the highest circles of the land, one who could dine with the Duke of Wellington and the Prince Regent, a friend of Wordsworth, Coleridge and Southey. As probably the leading Scotsman of his day, he was invited to head the team which recovered the lost Regalia of Scotland in Edinburgh Castle. Shortly afterwards, in 1818, he was knighted. When George the Fourth visited Scotland, it was to Scott that he turned to plan the fitting pageantry of his tour. That romantic, idealised picture of Scotland, blossoming at the visit of the King, and re-echoing through the reigns of Victoria and her successors to this day, owes so much to Scott and his writings. Visitors to Edinburgh still arrive at the railway station, named 'Waverley' after his novel, and as they walk along Princes Street, below the Castle, will find themselves drawn to Scott's monument at its heart.

Sir Walter Scott, though, was not merely a man of letters, confined to his study at Abbotsford. He was a sociable man, who loved to travel. In 1815, after the defeat of Napoleon at Waterloo, he planned with great excitement, a visit to the Continent. The six week tour included Holland and Belgium, a visit to the battlefield and to Paris where Wellington still resided as the Hero of Waterloo.

It was on his return to England that he visited Derbyshire. Had we met him in the streets of Castleton, we would have seen a tall, vigorous man, with a limping walk. Portraits such as those by Sir Henry Raeburn and Colvin Smith, and written descriptions, show a high forehead with fair to light brown hair cut straight across his brow. He had a fresh complexion and blue eyes. Those who conversed with him told of a thoughtful expression, except when speaking, for then his features lit up with animation. He had a great capacity for friendship – the names of those among whom he moved, from monarch to humblest shepherd, crowd the years from his childhood onwards.

It was one of these, a Border neighbour called Robert Scott of Gala, who accompanied Walter to the Continent. On their return, they landed at Brighton and then travelled northwards by coach to Abbotsford, visiting Dovedale and Castleton, with descents into Peak and Speedwell Caverns, on the way. Memories of his time in the Peak District must have lingered in his mind. Certainly, the name of the castle, 'Peveril of the Peak', fired his imagination, for it became the title of his longest novel, published in 1823. The story is set in the aftermath of the Civil War, a 'Romeo and Juliet' tale of romance and adventure,and feuding Cavalier and Roundhead families. The action swiftly moves from Derbyshire to London and the Isle of Man. But Martindale Castle is probably modelled on Haddon Hall. If one visited the Hall and then reads the novel, one can see the connections. The Peveril great hall with its dais, gallery and long table, and the adjoining bedroom with its cornice of boars' heads and peacocks certainly appear to be echoes of Haddon.

Sadly, though, Sir Walter Scott's life did not end in fame and fortune. Over the years, he had engaged in publishing, and in 1809, had become the half-owner of the John Ballantyne Publishing Company, later bought by Archibald Constable and Company. In 1826, after the collapse of the publishers, he became insolvent. For a man of honour, so steeped in the chivalric code of the past, he felt it incumbent upon him to repay his creditors. All his future income, he pledged, would be paid to a trust. He wrote tirelessly to attempt to repay his

Castleton Church from the south

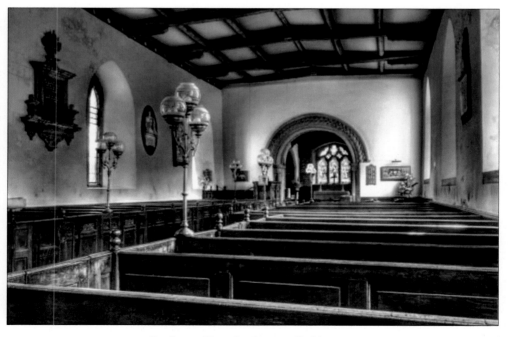

Castleton Church, the nave looking east

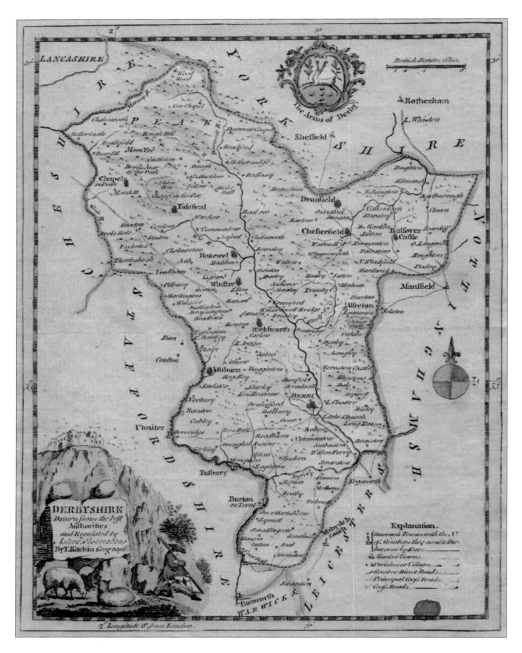

debts. In that same year, his wife died. Stress and overwork sapped his energies over the next three years. In 1832, he returned to Abbotsford from a visit to Italy, and died in his home. Sir Walter Scott is buried in Dryburgh Abbey.

He was one among so many who came to Castleton, and were

inspired by its natural wonders and its antiquity. It is a place which attracts at two levels. On the surface, it is a lively village with a holiday atmosphere. Walkers set off from its walls, to ramble among the towering hills, and coaches disgorge excited schoolchildren on field trips. But below the surface is the other Castleton – a mysterious world of caves and stalactites and mines .

Visitors have come to the village from all over the world. Why not add to their number? Buses from Sheffield and Bakewell bring one easily to Castleton. They all pass through glorious Peak District scenery, but perhaps the most delightful is that from Bakewell. Bus 173, run by Hulleys of Baslow, takes one from the gentle valley of the Wye, via Ashford in the Water with its picture-postcard bridge, to the higher hills. The road leads one through stone-built orderly villages such as Great Longstone with its green and Litton with its wide street. In the Spring, the verges are aglow with the gold of daffodils, the slopes gilded by the gleam of celandines. Stone walls 'tidy' the landscape into rooms, some rectangular and elongated in parallel lines to the horizon, others squared and neat alongside farmhouses. Sheep are dotted like limestone boulders, their lambs adding joyful life to the fields in the early months. The village of Tideswell is worth pausing to visit on the way, its magnificent, towered Church known as the 'Cathedral of the Peak'. If one sits on the left of the bus, one can look down into the Monsal Valley and see the viaduct so criticised by Ruskin, but surely serving as a frame for the scene. There are often ramblers here, as the Monsal Trail takes them across the viaduct. At Bradwell, one descends into Hope Valley, passing through villages such as Edale and Hope. All too soon after such beauty, the first houses of Castleton appear, and then a tantalising glimpse of the keep of Peveril of the Peak. The bus swings into its station, the main street of shops and cafés stretches invitingly ahead. As one walks down to the Visitors' Centre, or turns left to follow the stream towards Peak Cavern, the hills beckon. A road leads to Winnats Pass and the entrance to Speedwell Cavern. To follow the footpath beside it is to be led along one of the most entrancing ways in the country. Above soar the Gates of Winnats, to the right the rim of hills ascend to the crumbling cliff of Mam Tor. Colours change with seasons– dark greens of trees, russet bracken, emerald fields edged with grey stone walls, sometimes bleached and glistening with snow. The return walk opens out the panorama of Hope Valley like a wide screen, and – at its heart – lies the village of Castleton.

71

Photograph of Alison Uttley taken by her then fiancé
James Uttley c1911 on Wimbledon Common
© The University of Manchester

5. CROMFORD – MUCH MORE THAN MILLS

There are some places in the country where time seems to stand still. It is as though one walks straight into an eighteenth century engraving; or into a scene from a sepia photograph. Buildings have remained virtually unchanged. Trees may have grown, or been cut down. But walls and rooftops, and hills sloping to the horizon are timeless. One can almost hear the rumble of a stage-coach round the next bend. Or

Hand coloured engraving of Cromford c1860, by Newman & Co, London, published by W. Bemrose & Son, Derby

picture top-hatted gentlemen or long-skirted ladies about to appear round the next corner.

Cromford is such a place.

To enter it, is to step back into a village as it was two hundred years ago. Apart from busy traffic, and the modern conveniences of the twenty first century, its streets and houses are those from a time-slip.

For Cromford was largely the brain-child of one man, – Sir Richard Arkwright. Its houses and amenities were purpose-built to service his industry. Arkwright was responsible for the world's first successful water-powered cotton mill. He would become famous as the father of the factory system. Today, the community he developed is a World Heritage Site, and one of the best-preserved factory communities of the Industrial Revolution.

Before his arrival from Lancashire in 1771, Cromford was a village inhabited by a few lead-mining families. In the surrounding hills were sheep and dairy farms. He saw the potential of the area, for at Cromford, there was a reliable water source in the Bonsall Brook, good communications, and a ready labour force. The stage was set for the birth of the factory, where raw materials could enter at the beginning of the process, to emerge as manufactured goods. Although he claimed to have invented he water-powered cotton spinning frame, he probably 'improved' it. But he alone can be given the credit for organ-ising the labour and the water power necessary to realise its potential. In 1775, he obtained the patent for the revolutionary cotton carding machine. The former wig-maker evolved into the highly successful businessman. A visit to Derby Art Gallery brings one face to face with him, in a portrait by Joseph Wright. There he sits, wig on his head, a large proud gentleman. He has a surprisingly cherubic face for so aggressive and powerful man. Behind him is the secret of his power – the spinning frame! Painted in the same years (1789-90) is the life-size picture of Arkwright's son Richard Junior and his family. He continued his father's business success, but diversified too as a banker. In fact, in time he became the wealthiest untitled man in England. A comparison of the two portraits illustrates this. In contrast to his father's plain chair and clothes, Richard Junior and family are dressed in the height of fashion. What an amazing hat adorns the head of Mrs Arkwright! In that same year, too, Willersley Castle was built as their home – both portraits and house displaying their aspirations and position in society.

Today, then, we can reach Cromford easily from Derby using the

Trans Peak bus along the A6. Or, we can catch the 6.1 bus via Wirksworth. This will bring one down the steep hill and open panoramic views across to Riber Castle on the skyline. But, perhaps the most delightful way to travel is to take the train on the Derby to Matlock line, and to alight at Cromford Station. It is a gem, to which we will return later in our tour.

As we leave the station, on our right is the carriage drive to Willersley Castle. Sir Richard Arkwright lived in Rock House, over-looking his mill. But he had ambitions to build himself a castle. The original was destroyed by fire, but soon rebuilt. Arkwright, though, was destined never to live there – he died before its completion. It is now a Christian Guild Hotel, and is open to non-residents. The views from its long windows give sweeping glimpses of the Derwent Valley. The reception rooms are elegant, but the oval hall with its soaring stair-cases is certainly the most memorable part of the interior. If one stays overnight, then one can wander the grounds which rise steeply behind the Castle. There is even an indoor swimming pool! But, best of all, is to borrow an old key, for then you have the freedom to explore the wooded slopes leading down to the River, and you can surprise other visitors to Matlock Bath, by appearing through the gates between the private grounds and the Derwent Gardens!

We return, though, to the road from the station to the village. Ahead is the bridge across the Derwent. It is in two parts, with rounded arches upstream and Gothic pointed arches downstream. The bridge dates from the fifteenth century, and was no doubt the earliest crossing point here. 'Cromford' means 'crooked ford' and was mentioned in the Domesday Book. Perhaps this was its place of origin. Journeys were dangerous in those far-off days. So, it is little wonder that there are the remains of a chapel beside the bridge.

Views change, though, with the passing centuries. Next to the chapel, in the eighteenth century, different 'gods' were worshipped, and a Fishing Temple was built ! .

The road leads us onwards towards the mills. On the right is St. Mary's Church, another of Sir Richard's buildings. It began as a plain Georgian chapel in 1797. But in 1838, Peter Arkwright largely rebuilt it in the 'Gothic' style of the time. The tower was enlarged and the West End added, with an attractive arched entrance porch. The Church is rarely open, but it is worth enquiring at the Arkwright Mill. Inside are pleasing murals, showing scenes from the Bible.

Across the car park ahead, we are soon swallowed into the sturdy stone walls of Arkwright's Mill. Alongside the road, there are no windows on the lower floors. Indeed, it has a defensive, inward-looking atmosphere about it. Here we stand where History was made. Today, it is protected as the UNESCO World Heritage Site of the Derwent Valley Mills. The mill is quiet now, apart from the voices of visitors. But in its heyday, it would have been a noisy, bustling place, with the clatter of the machines. At its height, 1000 workers, many of them children, were employed here. Night and day, the mighty wheels turned and the machinery rolled out the endless bales of cotton to the waiting world.

Later in its history, the mill became silent as markets changed.

It became a dye factory, and then fell into disuse. The colossal buildings were empty – a sad reminder of past empires. Now, its story turns a new chapter. It has been rescued, and today is run by the Arkwright Society. Tours are possible around its great courtyard and its water wheels, and give a fascinating insight into life at the mill. Some of the buildings house shops, and there is an excellent café serving home-cooked lunches and cakes.

Across the road is the canal, built in 1792-94. Parallel to the Derwent, it runs for over 12 miles to Langley Mill. Barges and horses are gone long ago, but we can still see some of its structures at Cromford Wharf. Art exhibitions are often held in them, especially at the Derbyshire Open Studios days in the Summer. A barge had been

Masson Mill, Cromford

restored enabling visitors to have a gentle sail along the canal. It is an attractive place for a level walk in any season. But, come in the Autumn too, when the trees glow on the hillsides across the valley. At the end of the tow-path is Leawood Pumping Station, with its slender chimney. It was built in 1849 to raise water from the Derwent into the canal. Enthusiasts staff the pump several times a year, and it is thrilling to see it in steaming action. High Peak Junction marks the link between canal and railway. In the workshop there are relics of that industrial past, including reputedly rails from the oldest section of railway in the world. A steep path leads one to the line of the High Peak Railway, built in 1830. It is a climb, but if you can do it, you will be rewarded by stunning views .

But, let us return to the road by the Mill and retrace our steps to the A6. Further ahead is the imposing redbrick Masson Mill, Arkwright's show-piece, opened in 1783. Venetian windows adorn its façade. Nowadays, it houses a shopping centre and café. It is good to pause here for a coffee, as one is level with the rushing waters of the Derwent. Part of the complex still preserves the machinery in a museum. Here, it is fascinating to talk to people who once staffed its noisy machines. A few minutes with them will bring the old Mill to life and activity once more.

We return to the crossroads at the A6, and take the road ahead. It leads to the steep Cromford Hill. Well-built terraced stone cottages line it. At the foot of the hill stands the elegant Greyhound Hotel.

The Greyhound Hotel, Cromford

Scarthin Books, Cromford

Sir Richard Arkwright planned it, both to welcome businessmen and travellers, and to serve as a place of entertainment for the mill workers. In front, in the past, was the busy Market Place. Facing the Greyhound, one notices a narrow street to its right, leading behind it. This leads to 'Scarthin', and opens out into a quiet promenade with seats. Here, one soon finds a marvellous bookshop, named 'Scarthin' after the place. It is well worth a visit, although one must be wary of the passing of time inside! For it is one of those places where minutes slip away, unnoticed. One can enjoy a coffee, too, between the searches for that necessary book which one MUST have!

The bookshop faces the millpond, used originally to store water for the mills. It is pleasant to pause here, to soak up the sunshine, and watch the ducks. But after a rest, one returns to the Market Place, and

*North Street, Cromford, showing the terraced cottages
built by Sir Richard Arkwright in the 1770s*

*The Bell Inn on the corner of North Street,
Cromford*

turns right. Cross the road, and look for North Street. On either side are the stone, terraced cottages built by Sir Richard in the 1770s. for his workforce. The third storey of each is an indication of its use in the past when the top floors housed knitting frames. In fact, they are often to be seen in these Derbyshire villages. At the end of the street is the school, built in the 1830s. by Arkwright Junior. So, Cromford was constructed as a self-contained community, with houses, church, hotel, and workplace, – even tokens as its own currency for the workers. It is not difficult to picture them hurrying down the hill to be on time for their next shift. For so much has remained that the village is a window into the birth of the Industrial Revolution.

The waters of the Derwent have been channelled and stored. The rock at Scarthin Nick has been blasted away (in 1816), to push through the A6 from Derby to Matlock. The taming hand of man is apparent everywhere in the landscape, and yet, the wildness of Derbyshire, which first drew visitors here, encircles Cromford. Arkwright and his successors may have done their best to exploit the area and its resources for their industry. But, on the steep hillsides ,and among the villages, ancient rocks protrude. Towards Matlock, the sheer-sided cliffs form a gorge and Scarthin face creates a great wall to the sky After heavy rain, the Derwent is angry, and still floods downstream. Elm, ash and sycamore clothe the uplands. Under their protection, the flowers grow each Spring. Willow warblers, black cap haunt the woodlands. Pastures make emerald patterns between the groups of trees. A few farms structure the slopes, their sheep relieving the greenness with dots of white.

Let us, then, leave the industrial landscape of the eighteenth century, and return to the station. Alighting here is like taking a step into another country. For there is a French château-style station-

The waiting room at Cromford Station

master's house, and a Swiss chalet waiting room. They are believed to have been designed by G.H. Stokes, the son-in-law of Sir Joseph Paxton (designer of the Crystal Palace), and completed in 1849. Their inspiration must have been to provide a gateway to the Wonders of the Peak for those Victorian passengers.

On its platform in those years at the end of the nineteenth century would have stood a schoolgirl from a nearby farm. Her name was Alison Uttley. She lived at Castle Top Farm, and was on her way to Lady Manners School, Bakewell. Castle Top remains, a solid stone farmhouse on the hillside above Cromford. In September 2012, a blue plaque was unveiled there, to commemorate her childhood years.

Alison, known originally as Alice Jane Taylor, was born in 1884, at Castle Top, where her family had been tenant-farmers for generations. Her first school-days were spent at Lea School, Holloway, before she left to attend Lady Manners School, Bakewell. Here, her love of science lessons led to the ambition to study that subject at a deeper level. She obtained a scholarship, and went on to Manchester University, where she read Physics. Alison graduated in 1906, – only the second woman honours graduate at the University.

As an independently-minded young woman, she became a suffragette. Among her friends in these years she could include Ramsay MacDonald. Indeed, there is a tradition that his children were the first to hear her tell stories.

The practicalities of having to earn a living, and her enthusiasm to share her love of her subject, led to teacher training at Cambridge. A portrait painted from a photograph of her at this time shows a young woman with a strong face, her dark hair parted in the middle. Two years after graduation, Alison became a Physics teacher at Fulham Secondary School for Girls.

In 1911, she married James Arthur Uttley. They would have one son, called John. From 1924 to 1938, her home was at Bowden, Cheshire.

Then tragedy struck the family. James' health, like that of many other young men, had been affected by his experiences in the First World War. In 1930, he drowned himself. Alison was then left on her own, with a son to support as well, and so she decided to use her gift for writing stories to earn a living.

The first books were directly influenced by her love of the country-side, and were tales of animals as different 'human' characters. As she later wrote,"They are real. I didn't sit down to write a story, they came". The stories of Little Gray Rabbit, Red Fox, Sam Pig and other endearing creatures would become classics, loved by generations of children.

Later books were for older children and adults. One of the best-known is *A Traveller in Time*, in which the heroine Penelope goes to stay with her Aunt at 'Thackers' in Derbyshire. The house is modelled on the 16th century Manor House at Dethick in Derbyshire, near to Castle Top. It passed into the Babington family through marriage in 1423, and in the 16th century, its owner was Sir Anthony Babington, High Sheriff of the county. Sir Anthony had been a page in the household of the Earl of Shrewsbury, at the period when the Earl was the custodian of Mary, Queen of Scots. A combination of compassion for the captive Queen and his Catholic faith, a dangerous mix in the reign of Elizabeth the First, led to his involvement in a plot to assassinate Elizabeth and replace her with Mary on the throne of England. The conspiracy became known as the 'Babington Plot'. Babington was trapped, with his fellow-plotters, and was executed for treason. Penelope, then, during her stay in the house, finds herself slipping to and fro in time, to 1582, and witnesses the events unfolding to their final tragic ending. It is a highly-imaginative novel, and was made into a television series in 1978.

Alison in fact wrote over a hundred books. During the war, she moved to Beaconsfield, Buckinghamshire, where she named her house 'Thackers' after the one in her novel. A near neighbour was fellow-children's writer, Enid Blyton. Only one meeting is recorded between the two ladies. It happened at the local fishmonger's, and Alison was very dismissive of the author in her diaries! These were kept for over forty years, and were published in 2009. They reveal a different aspect of Alison from the well-loved children's writer. She appears in them as a complex, emotional personality. Although a trained scientist, she was also a mystic, holding life-long beliefs in fairies and time travel, and believing that people could move between different worlds.

Professor Denis Judd in his biography, wrote,"Though she ended her life as a grande dame of literature, she was acclaimed, but never entirely content".

The most familiar portrait of her, though, shows her in thoughtful pose as the famous writer, gazing into the distance, chin on hand and book on knee. Her silver hair is formally-styled, and waved back from a high forehead. A smart black dress and rows of pearls complete the picture of the 'lady of letters'. This is no doubt how she would wish us to see her, to forget her darker side and instead to remember her as the 'spinner' of well-loved children's books .

Alison Uttley may have left Derbyshire to go to Manchester University, and later to live in Cheshire and Buckinghamshire, but she never forgot her native county. *A Traveller in Time* and the *Little Grey Rabbit* books drew on the countryside she remembered and loved. In her writings, she would return to its well-loved hills again and again.

But it is Cromford which remained especially dear in her memory. These were the days of steam trains, – of Cromford Station staffed by a station-master and porter, of flower-filled gardens, and the transport of milk in churns from the farms.

Alison was a true 'railway child', who watched for the trains to emerge from Willersley Tunnel and waved to the passengers. She had a red leather season ticket – part of her scholarship to the school. The guard wore a button-hole, and kept a kindly eye on the schoolgirls. In the Winter, iron hot water bottles were provided, to warm passengers' feet, and coal fires blazed in the waiting room. It must have seemed full of home comforts. There was even a polished table with flowers in a bowl and a Bible. Those were the days!

Two of Alison Uttley's books convey her memories of a childhood in Cromford. *Our Village* is a collection of essays which vividly bring to life the people and places of the community.

The Country Child is a novel, the story of Susan Garland growing up on the farm called Windystone Hall. For 'Susan Garland', we may read Alison Uttley; for 'Windystone Hall', Castle Top Farm. It is a book in which memory and imagination are so closely interwoven that one hardly knows where one ends and the other begins – a carpet whose threads are so twisted together that to pull out one would be to destroy

the pattern. The events in Susan's life do not happen in chronological order. Instead, each chapter is a 'photograph', the kind of picture we have from events in our childhood. Not all are happy or idyllic. Susan's lonely walks from school take her through the Dark Wood, where 'They' lurk to terrify her with fears she cannot put into words. On the first days at the village school, she is bullied.

But her world is an ordered, generally contented one, too. It is a world of passing, unhurried seasons, of festivals celebrated in church and farm, of the yard dog Roger and the wild creatures of the hills, of stirring the milk and baking in the warm kitchen which was the heart of the house. Lively personalities crowd her pages. There is the servant girl Betty ,who can bake, brew and make perfect butter. Another helper on the farm is old Joshua who knew how to care for the animals. Others come and go – Eli the travelling rat-catcher, Michael who came from Galway to help with the harvest, and the girl who rode the pony in the circus.

Dominating and cradling everyone, though, is the countryside. It is a dream landscape, observed in wonderful detail. Passing storms, the scents of Autumn with its mushrooms and fallen ferns, the hopeful colours of the Spring blossoms, the snow deep as only childhood snow can be – Alison Uttley remembers and describes them lovingly, the landscapes of her memory.

A Country Child is a book to dip into, or perhaps to read after a walk in the Derbyshire hills. But the essays bring us face to face with Cromford itself. One can take the book with one, and trace the shops she visited in today's houses.

If we begin at the A6 crossroads, on the left would have been the flour mill and forge. From there to North Street were the butcher, bonnet shop, grocer and post office. Young Alison delighted most in the newsagent's. Mr Brown sold newspapers, but also toys, saucepans, books and 'lucky bags'. There was no greengrocer as people grew their own vegetables. Nor cake shop, as it was home baking in those days.

One of the most intriguing shops sounds to have been the tinsmith's, owned by a Miss Kidd, who sold lanterns, brushes and baking-tins. Around the Market Place were grouped the cobbler, saddler, tailor and bootmaker. Cromford must have been a miniature world to those who lived there – a generally self-sufficient one.

It was in the Market Place, in front of the Greyhound, that the Wakes fair was held in late Summer. It must have seemed like Heaven to a child! There were stalls to explore, a merry go round, and swing boats.

Alison would buy peppermint rock and gingerbread men, and the special spiced 'Wakes cakes'. It was a Saturday to enjoy – a happy break for the hard-working farmers and trades people of Cromford.

Her descriptions of the Wakes and Christmas in the village Church probably best sum up the pleasure of those distant days.

As she wrote: "To our own ivy-covered church, we entered at Christmas in a spirit of excitement and wonder, eager to see the beauty, the transformation to a woodland as it seemed to me; and with senses alert and eyes wide we stared at the flowers and berries, we breathed in the fragrance of the evergreens".

Cromford!

Cover of The Private Diaries of Alison Uttley edited by Denis Judd
© Denis Judd, showing a portrait of Alison Uttley and drawings by Margaret Tempest

A first visit here cannot be one's last!

Its attractions lure one to the village again and again.

One can begin as an 'historian', to see for oneself the achievements of Arkwright and explore this cradle of the Industrial Revolution.

Alison Uttley's writings will weave their subtle magic and carry one back to the days of her youth. Book in hand, one can climb the steep street and discover the shops she knew.

Railway enthusiasts can marvel at the pump house, and at the engineers who built the early railway.

A summer afternoon can be whiled away under the shade of Derwent's trees.

Or there can be the brisk walk along the Canal in the first frosts.

All this in one small village in Derbyshire?

One visit surely can never be enough!

Portrait of Charlotte Bronte, by J.H. Thompson 1850s
By kind permission of The Bronte Society

6. THE HATHERSAGE OF CHARLOTTE BRONTE – THE 'MORTON' OF 'JANE EYRE'

Like the battlements of a castle, the ridge of Stanage Edge looms over Hathersage, its rim against the sky-line seemingly fashioned by giant hands at the whim of some mediaeval lord. In Summer, the slopes skirting Stanage blaze with purple heather. In the Autumn, they are bronzed with bracken and long grass, as though preparations are being made for a tournament, with banners unfurled beneath the walls. But the ramparts of Stanage are not man-made. They are of grey millstone,

Engraving of drawing of Hathersage 1886, by T.C. Hofland

hard and unyielding where softer rock has been eroded around it.

There is a magnetism about that horizon. Eyes are drawn upwards, to where sky meets stone. Lower down, ferns give way to grass and trees and hedges. Steep-sided hills race down into Hope Valley, their fields dotted by sheep, like stones scattered from the ridge above. The hills overlap and enfold, making patterns of shaded greens and dry-grass golds.

It was on one of these, on a natural spur looking back to Stanage, that the original Hathersage developed. The name is Saxon – 'Hereseige' or 'Ridge settlement'. Nothing remains from that distant age, but one can certainly still see the work of Norman hands. Massive grass-covered earthworks at Camp Green show where a fortification once stood, overshadowing the earliest houses clustering at its foot, and the valley below.

Since then, over the centuries, the village has spread downwards, towards the Derwent, where streams zigzag their courses across the valley floor. Houses were generally confined to one main street through which pack horse teams wended their way.

By the eighteenth century, Hathersage had its fair share of local industries. Mills made productive use of the water. Brass buttons, wire, needles and pins were manufactured here. Stagecoaches from Sheffield and the Derbyshire towns passed through its street, and stopped outside the George Inn

On a June day in 1845, a young lady was waiting eagerly at the Inn for the coming of the 'omnibus' coach. Her name was Miss Ellen Nussey and she was staying for a few weeks at the Vicarage where her brother Henry was Vicar. He, though, was away on his honeymoon, and Ellen was here to prepare the house for the newly-wedded couple.

But it was not for their arrival that she waited with such anticipation.

It was that of her friend from school-days, Miss Charlotte Bronte, who had been invited by the family to spend three weeks at the Vicarage, – ostensibly to help with the preparations, but also to keep Ellen company and to enjoy a holiday together.

So, what had brought them together in the years before their visit to Derbyshire?

Charlotte was born, and lived for most of her life, at the Parsonage in Haworth, Yorkshire. She was the daughter of the Reverend Patrick Bronte, originally from County Down and his Cornish-born wife Maria. They had six children, – a son Branwell, and daughters Maria, Elizabeth, Charlotte, Emily and Anne. Sadly though, their mother died when Charlotte was only six, and her aunt Elizabeth Branwell then came to care for the children. The girls' education outside the home began at Cowan Bridge School, fifty miles from Haworth, where Maria and Elizabeth became terminally ill, and from where their father soon removed their sisters. These were devastating times for the family, later remembered by Charlotte in the unhappy childhood of Jane Eyre at 'Lowood'.

Her next school was Roe Head, Mirfield near Huddersfield, and it was here that she met Ellen Nussey, who would become her life-long friend and correspondent.

Charlotte wrote of Ellen that she was, "a conscientious, observant, calm, well-bred Yorkshire girl". She said of her, "No friend – could be

to me what Ellen is".

They visited each others' homes, and corresponded regularly. Ellen's family lived at The Rydings, Birstall, West Yorkshire, a few miles from Bradford. It is an attractive stone house, with large windows and castellated rooftops, and probably became in part the model for 'Thornfield' in *Jane Eyre*. Later, the Nussey family moved to nearby Brookroyd, and it was here, in 1848, that Charlotte corrected the proofs for *Jane Eyre*.

Ellen's family had made their wealth from cloth-manufacturing, and for her, life was lived in a comfortable family home. For Charlotte, however, the future was very different. She had gone to Roe Head School as a pupil when she was fifteen, and returned home for two years to teach Emily and Anne. At the age of nineteen, she went back to Roe Head, this time as a teacher. Then, after three years, she left again to become a governess.

She had ambitions, and it was to further these, that, in 1842, she and Emily went to study at the Pensionnat Heger in Brussels. Her plan was to improve fluency in French, and to learn Italian and German, so that, with the background of a wider education, she and Emily could open their own school.

They travelled to Brussels in February, and returned home when their Aunt died. Emily then remained at Haworth to look after their father and the house. Charlotte, though, made the fateful decision to go back alone to the Pensionnat Heger, this time as a teacher.

That year in Brussels was to have the most profound effect on her life and writings. For Charlotte fell deeply in love with her charismatic professor Constantin Heger. It was a hopeless love, for Monsieur Heger was a happily-married family man.

In January, to escape from an intolerable situation, a wounded Charlotte came home. But she wrote to him. Her letters, revealing something of her torment and her passionate feelings, have been preserved. In one she wrote, 'I will tell you candidly that during this time of waiting, I have tried to forget you – and when one has suffered this kind of anxiety for one or two years, one is ready to do anything to regain peace of mind'.

There were no replies from Brussels.

Yet, Charlotte did receive several proposals of marriage. In 1839, a young Irish clergyman, called Mr Price, visited the Parsonage at Haworth, and obviously enjoyed her company. Within a few days, he sent a letter of proposal to Charlotte.

As Charlotte wrote to Ellen, "Well! thought I, I have heard of love at first sight, but this beats all". There was no return of his infatuation, and she heard a few months later, the sad news that Mr Price had died.

Her second suitor was James Taylor, who was sent by the firm of publishers who employed him, to collect the manuscript of Charlotte's novel *Shirley*. He was a capable, intelligent man, who from her letters to Ellen, seems to have awakened Charlotte's interest. His first visit took place in September 1849, and there were exchanges of letters and books. But any initial feelings for him on Charlotte's part soon wore off. In April 1851, she wrote to Ellen, "the lines of his face show an inflexibility, and I must add, a hardness of character which do not attract". She added, "If Mr Taylor be the only husband fate offers to me, single I must always remain."

Shortly afterwards, he left for India, on business for the publishers. Charlotte had already died before his eventual return in 1856.

What, then, was Charlotte's appearance?

There are three known portraits of her – the painting by her brother Branwell of the three sisters, a portrait by J.H. Thompson, and a chalk drawing by George Richmond. The latter two certainly are flattering. Thompson's shows her gleaming light brown hair and oval face, while Richmond's portrays a grave, thoughtful face framed by full, smooth hair parted in the middle over a high forehead. Contemporaries describe her soft, silky hair and beautiful grey eyes. But they also mention a sallow complexion and lack of height (she was four foot ten). She was very short-sighted; her round spectacles are preserved in her writing desk. In company, she was very shy and reserved, but blossomed within the circle of her family and closest friends. Her letters reveal a charm and liveliness, and a flow of words which must surely have been echoed in eloquent conversation.

Charlotte had a third admirer, from within that close circle of friends. He was Ellen's brother Henry Nussey, who had known her over the years from her visits to his sister. Henry was a clergyman, and in March 1839, was curate at Donnington. He was eager to establish a school there, and began to consider the possibility of a wife to look after the children. His thoughts turned to Charlotte, and he wrote to propose to her.

She did not delay her reply. In a letter to Ellen, she divulged, it had been a decided negative! Charlotte esteemed him, as a friend, and there was the attraction of his being brother to Ellen. But, as she wrote to Henry, "Mine is not the sort of disposition calculated to form the happiness of a man like you – You do not know me. I am not the serious, grave, cool-headed individual you suppose; you would think me romantic and eccentric, satirical and severe."

She confided in Ellen that she did not love him. She "could not have that intense attachment which would make me willing to die for him." That was the ultimate test for her.

Six months later, he was to be congratulated on finding a suitable wife. They continued to correspond as friends for the next two years, but by January 1841, the letters came to an end.

All this, of course, was in the past when Charlotte accepted the invitation to come to Hathersage. The years at school, the months as governess, the proposals from Mr Price and Henry Nussey, the early writings, and the heart-break of unrequited love for Professor Heger had happened before that summer. Perhaps Charlotte revealed some of her sadness to Ellen, but we do not know whether she did, or chose to remain silent.

The invitation certainly would be a welcome respite from the family responsibilities, and from all that had happened in Brussels. Ellen was away from the family home. Charlotte was too. She was able to leave her father in the care of Emily and Anne, while Ellen's mother stayed at Brookroyd. They were two young women looking forward to their independent holiday in Hathersage, probably delighting in the thought of freedom to do what they wished for a while. So, although there were the preparations to be made, time was their own to sit in the garden and chat, to visit parishioners, or to roam the hills.

For around the Vicarage were footpaths leading through the fields to the encircling moors. And surely those moors drew Charlotte, as they did at home in Haworth. There was time, then, to store-up names and houses and scenery, to be distilled and evoked through imagination in her later writings.

In June 1845, she finished the novel *The Professor*, based on her life in Brussels. Then in August, during a visit to Manchester with her father for his cataract operation, she began *Jane Eyre*.

In the novel, the troubled heroine, fleeing from Mr Rochester after discovering that he already has a wife, finds refuge at the home of the Rivers sisters in the village of Morton. Their brother St. John, a clergyman, provides work for Jane at a local school, and later proposes to her, seeing her as a suitable wife and companion for his work as a missionary. Perhaps memories of Henry, who too sought Charlotte as his wife, became focussed and sharpened in the character of the ascetic St. John. For both Charlotte and Jane had known the reality of a deeper love in their passion for Professor Heger and Mr Rochester. Certainly, Morton itself is a temporary sanctuary for Jane, – a positive reflection perhaps of the peaceful holiday at Hathersage after the trauma of Brussels.

The evidence for the connection is convincing. Names from the neighbourhood pepper the chapters set in Morton, The landlord of the George Inn where she had alighted from the coach was a Mr Morton. The same surname appears too on the charity boards in the Church tower.

In the Church is a splendid collection of brasses and monuments from the fifteenth and sixteenth centuries. They commemorate the Eyre family who were local landowners. Indeed, seven halls in the area were built by its members.

One of these houses is called 'North Lees', situated in the valley above Hathersage, and sheltered by Stanage Edge. In *Jane Eyre*, the name of Mr Rochester's home is 'Thornfield'. A rearrangement of the letters of 'thorn' give 'north', while 'lee' is the old name for 'field'. According to local tradition, at one time in its distant past, a woman called Agnes Ashurst was reputedly lodged in a padded room in the house, as she suffered from madness, and perished there in a fire. In

Charlotte's imagination, did the unhappy woman become the lunatic wife of Mr Rochester, kept for safety in the attics of Thornfield? At the time of Charlotte's visit, too, there was an ornate cupboard in the house, called 'The Apostles' Cupboard', a description of which appears in the novel.

In *Jane Eyre*, the wealthy man who financially supports the village school at Morton is a Mr Oliver, whose father was a 'journeyman needle-maker'. The surname is in the Church registers and, as has been seen, needle-making was a local industry.

After her wanderings across the moors, Jane found safety at Moor House, the home of the Rivers' sisters. The Moor House, or 'Moorseats' of today, nestles among protective trees under steep hillsides and looks out across the Hope Valley. It was another Eyre property, owned by various members of the family over the years, and sometimes let out to tenants, as it seems to have been at the time of Charlotte's visit. In 1855, it was bought by Thomas Eyre, who considerably extended the house. But in 1845, it was still a moorland farmhouse, built in the fifteenth century and enlarged in the seventeenth. So the Moorseats known to Charlotte and Ellen would have been a gabled small manor house, surrounded by a garden and extensive woodland. One of the out-buildings, with its pointed arch, may have been a chapel, in the days when the Eyre family followed their Catholic faith. There is a tradition of at least one visit paid by the two ladies to the house that summer. If so, it would have been a delightful walk, not far from the Vicarage, across meadows bright with buttercups.

There were so many happy memories for Charlotte Bronte to store up and reflect on after her return from Hathersage. Those memories would be honed and fired by her imagination, and so become the setting for the idyll with the Rivers family and Jane's eventual return to find her beloved Mr Rochester. As Charlotte wrote, "Reader, I married him."

In the years to come, Charlotte, too, would find a fleeting happiness through her marriage to her father's curate, William Bell Nicholls. As she wrote to Ellen, "I find in my husband the tenderest nurse, the kindest support, the best earthly comfort that ever woman had." Sadly, it was to be all too short, for Charlotte died in 1855, in the early stages of pregnancy. Among her last recorded words were, "We have been so happy."

Let us now visit, then, today's Hathersage, and look for traces of the village known to Charlotte. For to be there, is to be aware of her quiet presence, and that of her heroine, 'Jane Eyre'. They are inextricably interwoven. A paragraph in a guide-book, a sentence on a postcard, noticeboards,even though faded, call her into the present.

Stagecoaches and packhorse disappeared long ago. Instead, traffic rushes through the main street towards Sheffield or Castleton. Pavements in the summer months, are thronged with ramblers and day visitors, brought here by car, by bus from Bakewell, or by train from Sheffield. But much remains to remind us of the Hathersage as it was in the mid-nineteenth century.

We turn aside from that main street with its shops and cafés, and take the alley leading into Baulk Lane. In a few seconds, centuries fall away, and we are in the peace of the valley leading to Stanage Edge. Past the cricket pitch, a footpath climbs steeply across a couple of fields. We can already see the church spire and Vicarage, half hidden among tall trees.

It is worthwhile to pause for a few minutes in the Churchyard. For one grave has long been marked as the burial-place of Little John, faithful companion of Robin Hood. In the eighteenth century, the thigh bone of a man, estimated to have been about seven foot tall, was found here. At one time, so the story goes, his cap and bow hung inside the church. The traditional site of his cottage, east of the Church, can still be seen. In those days of long-ago, Sherwood Forest stretched as far as here, and many places in the area bear the name of Robin Hood. So, although precise facts are lost in the mists of time, the local, rather fascinating, stories linger.

The present Church dates from the fourteenth century, with a fifteenth centruy tower and clerestory, but the site is much older. Sunlight slants through the stained glass windows and polishes the glimmer of the Eyre brasses in the fifteenth century chantry chapel. The men are dressed in spectacular armour and their fashionable ladies, in trailing gowns and gabled headdresses. Above them is a Kempe east window, rescued from Derwent Church, now drowned beneath the waters of Ladybower Reservoir.

Outside again, we walk to the car park next to the modern vicarage, and look across the valley to Stanage. The walls of the old Vicarage, where Charlotte stayed, tell the story of its many phases of building. Documents record a house called 'The Vicarage' in the seventeenth century, but there have been many additions, some by Henry Nussey himself. As we retrace our path across the fields, we can look back and see the Vicarage, a solidly-built stone residence, with its bay windows

The old vicarage at Hathersage where Charlotte Bronte stayed with her friend Ellen Nussey

and chimneyed rooftops among the sheltering trees.

We continue to the valley floor and turn right, away from Hathersage. As we cross the meadows, we can imagine Charlotte and Ellen here too. Soon, all we can see of the village is the church spire, enfolded by the grassy slopes. Hedges terrace them. Woods grow more densely on the sky-line. The path is steep now, and becomes a drive. There, under the hill, lies North Lees. It is a three-storeyed tower house of warm grey stone, and dates from the sixteenth century. The top is battlemented and large latticed windows stare down into the valley. Behind it is an earlier tower, with four floors of smaller rooms. To the right is a later addition, a house in itself, but dwarfed by the height of the Hall. Remote and strongly-raised, it is the perfect setting for Mr Rochester's home. On its walled-about, flat roof, the heroine Jane Eyre could easily walk, and Mr Rochester's crazed wife fall to her death. Charlotte described it clearly as "a gentleman's manor house – surrounded by quiet and lonely hills, seeming to enclose Thornfield." Surely, this must be an echo of North Lees in its dramatic setting.

We leave North Lees brooding in its solitude, summoned by the

The 'new' vicarage at Hathersage

Hathersage Church, burial place of the Eyres

North Lees Hall

chime of Church bells. Jane Eyre, too, "turned in the direction of their sound." The Hathersage of Charlotte's time is all around us, although sometimes secluded or altered. The mills she saw still exist, now houses and offices. The site of the old school at Coggers Lane may be the one in Charlotte's mind as she described Jane's time there as school-mistress.

Moor House, now called Moorseats, is a private house, but its setting evokes Jane's arrival at the Rivers' home, struggling towards its kitchen window, like a moth towards light. The George Inn, too, remains at the heart of the bustling traffic of today, just as it was in 1845.

There is so much to be discovered in Hathersage. Its buildings ,and the names of their occupants, speak to us of Charlotte Bronte and her heroine. Her genius transformed the village into Morton, where Jane Eyre found a refuge. Charlotte walked its paths, stayed at its Vicarage, and worshipped in its Church. For three summer weeks, it was the setting for a holiday, free from all ties, when imagination could soar and memories crystallise.

But like us today, her gaze must often have been drawn to that ridge on the horizon, where Stanage stretched away from the safe valley to the wild and desolate moors.

The interior of Hathersage Church looking west

The last words should be hers – powerfully conjuring the Derbyshire landscape.

"There are great moors behind and on each hand of me; there are waves of mountains far beyond that deep valley at my feet. The population here must be thin, and I see no passengers on these roads; they stretch out east, west, north and south – white, broad, lonely; they are all cut in the moor, and the heather grows deep and wild to their very verge" (*Jane Eyre* Chapter 28).

John Ruskin
WA 2013.67 John Everett Millais, 'John Ruskin' © Ashmolean Museum, University of Oxford

7. MATLOCK BATH –
CHILDHOOD PARADISE OF JOHN RUSKIN

If we had to paint a portrait of John Ruskin, we probably would wish to picture him as the Sage of Brantwood, seated in his garden there and gazing out over the waters of Coniston in the Lake District; or pacing the palaces of Venice, sketchbook in hand. The artist Millais portrayed him in majestic pose, as he stands on the edge of the wild foaming waters of a Highland torrent. These seem the logical settings for the great Victorian.

But Derbyshire?

*The High Tor near Matlock Derbyshire, engraving by Thomas Allom
and J.W. Lowry, original 1836, hand coloured print c1845*

It is not a connection which we would readily make, apart from that one telling reference in his writings to Monsul Dale, and the railway piercing its heart. But Ruskin visited the county regularly, from his childhood onwards, and he loved it.

Carved into the wall of the Tourist Information Office at Castleton are two of his sayings. They describe Derbyshire as "the most educational of all English landscapes", and as a "lovely child's first alphabet".

If we had the ability to turn the clock back and see him on one of his visits to the county, he would appear as a slim, wiry gentleman, 5'9" in height. His face was thin, with a wide mouth. A student who heard him lecture at Oxford, described his brilliant, piercing blue eyes. The sideburns shown in so many of his earlier portraits, were augmented by a long beard after 1878. He was distinctively dressed, in a double-breasted waistcoat, frock coat with a high collar and a blue neck cloth.

Before following him, though, and considering his nostalgic love of the county, we should introduce ourselves to Ruskin himself. For in the early to middle part of the twentieth century, he rather fell out of fashion and became a somewhat neglected Victorian, a man of a past age. When compared to the flamboyant Pre-Raphaelites and their circle, he seemed to appear staid and dull. Yet, it was Ruskin who championed them in the early years of the Brotherhood, when it was unfashionable to do so. He was, indeed, a revolutionary, a strong and leading influence in so many areas, in his own lifetime, and beyond.

On the cover of Kevin Jackson's book *The Worlds of John Ruskin*, it states that he was "one of the most influential and exhilarating writers in England". Ruskin wrote over two hundred and fifty books and pamphlets, which were collected into thirty eight huge volumes. Among his greatest works were the five volumes of *Modern Painters* (1843-1860), *Seven Lamps of Architecture* (1849), *The Stones of Venice* in three volumes (1851-1853), *Unto this last* (1862), and *Fors Clavigera* (1871-1884). As Jackson concludes, with a plea, "Some of his prose is plain as a children's book or a Bible, some as intricate as a Persian tapestry. Almost all of it shines with ardent life and quicksilver intelligence, and a few passages are among the most beautiful ever achieved in the English language. Please read him".

Those writings influenced people from many different backgrounds. In 1904, the young lawyer Mohondas (Mahatma) Gandhi was travelling on an overnight train from Johannesburg to Durban. A friend had loaned him Ruskin's *Unto This Last* to read en route, and its words inspired him so much that he later wrote: "I was determined to change my life in accordance with the ideas of the book. I arose with the dawn determined to reduce their principles to practice".

World history can be said to have been changed as a result!

Leo Tolstoy believed Ruskin to be, "One of the most remarkable men, not only of England and our time, but of all countries at all times, he was of those rare men who think with their hearts".

For the novelist Henry James, he was, "the author of the most splendid pages in our language", while the art historian Kenneth Clark, who was a successor to Ruskin as Slade Professor at Oxford, described him as, "the best watercolourist of the second half of the nineteenth century".

Like Leonardo da Vinci and Erasmus Darwin, John Ruskin (1819 – 1900) was a polymath, a multi-faceted genius. He was a man of catholic interests, an inspiring writer on many subjects, and a passionate supporter of many causes.

Ruskin, though, is probably best remembered as an art critic and historian. He was the first Slade Professor of Fine Art at Oxford. Both Art and Architecture fascinated him, and he would have significant influence on the later Gothic Revival.

In addition, he was a social reformer, and a commentator on the environment. His 1884 lecture, 'The Storm-Cloud of the Nineteenth Century', has come to be seen as remarkably prophetic of recent thinking on pollution and climate change.

It was not only his writings, but his lectures too, which proved influential to his contemporaries. "To you", Oscar Wilde wrote, "the gods gave eloquence such as they have given to none other".

Such was his impact then. Nowadays, he is still remembered through, among others, Ruskin College, Oxford (named in his honour), the Ruskin Foundation and Library at Lancaster University, and a number of Ruskin Societies.

A fitting legacy for such a man!

John Ruskin was born in 1819 in Hunter Street, Bloomsbury, near the present-day St. Pancras Station. His father, John James Ruskin was a successful importer of sherry. His mother Margaret brought him up to read the Bible aloud every morning. It was their fondest, unfulfilled, hope that he would enter the Church, but although this was not to be, the family's reasonable wealth offered the means to indulge and support a gifted child.

From Hunter Street, they later moved to other London homes in Herne Hill and Denmark Hill; indeed, Ruskin would continue to use his study at Denmark Hill even after his mother's death in 1871 – John James died in 1864 – when the lease was given to his cousin Joan.

Summers, though, were for travelling. Two visits were made to Scotland by the time he was five, and their first continental trip was in 1825, to France and Belgium, including the battlefield of Waterloo. The journeys must have been delightful, made before the age of train and traffic, in their private high carriage. Derbyshire and the Lake District were visited in 1829 and 1837. Wherever he went, his hotel room would become his study, for Ruskin was already writing poems and plays from the age of seven.

In 1837, he became a student at Christ Church Oxford: as a Fellow Commoner he was not obliged to sit examinations, but did so anyway, graduating in 1842.

The next year, he began his first major work, – Volume One of *Modern Painters*, largely a defence and celebration of the work of J.M.W. Turner. Following two unsuccessful relationships and encouraged by his parents, in 1842, he married Effie Gray. Theirs would be a troubled, ill-fated marriage and was annulled six years later. Within a year, Effie had married John Everett Millais, the artist who had painted Ruskin's portrait on the Scottish holiday which had brought them together.

Over the years, through his writings and lectures, his fame and influence grew.

Ruskin's love of travel continued throughout his life; most years saw visits to France, Switzerland and Italy, until 1888 and the years darkened by illness. Brantwood, that delightful house overlooking Lake Coniston, was bought in 1871 and would become his later refuge until his death in 1900. It is open to the public and maintained by the Brantwood Trust. To one of the most famous men of his age, burial in Westminster Abbey was offered, but he lies modestly in Coniston churchyard.

And so to Derbyshire, visited in his childhood, with his wife Effie in 1851, and in his middle years. It was for him, a county to be viewed with nostalgia, one of those places from childhood where we imagine the days were always sunny. Memories of idyllic holidays no doubt influenced his passionate denunciation of the coming of the railways.

In Letter Five of *Fors Clavigera*, dated 1 May, 1871, he pictured the Derbyshire valley between Buxton and Bakewell as one in which the

*Monsal Dale "Now, every fool in Buxton can be at Bakewell
in half an hour, and every fool in Bakewell at Buxton"*

pagan gods might walk. Then came the railway striding across
Monsul Dale! He raged against its builders:

"You Enterprised a Railroad through the valley – you blasted its
rocks away, heaped thousands of tons of shale into its lovely stream.
The valley is gone, and the Gods with it; and now, every fool in
Buxton can be at Bakewell in half an hour, and every fool in Bakewell
at Buxton". A cry from the heart, part anger against the advance of
transport, part sadness for those nostalgic memories of the travels of
his youth.

Perhaps, though, he would be reassured if he returned today. The
viaduct remains, and seems to frame the valley. Walkers and cyclists
now enjoy the peaceful countryside; and, perhaps, ancient gods walk
once more at dawn across its fields...

He had practical plans, too, for Derbyshire. As part of the
programme for the Guild of St. George – still flourishing today – in
1875, he established the setting up of a museum for local workers, in
Walkley near Sheffield. It would house collections to illustrate the
natural history of the region – especially the geology and flora of
Derbyshire.

The family often stayed at the New Bath Hotel in Matlock Bath. A
sketch of 1871, possibly the view from near the hotel where Ruskin

wrote Letter Eight of *Fors Clavigera*, shows how charming the Derwent Valley must have been before the roar of the A6 traffic. But it was in that same year, while he was staying there, that Ruskin became seriously ill. Fortunately, there were caring friends to look after him and eventually, he recovered. He must have been a difficult, demanding patient. On one occasion, he requested some cold roast beef and mustard – at 2 am! There was none in the hotel, but after a search in nearby inns, the food was found. It came, wrapped in paper. Let us hope Ruskin enjoyed it!

The New Bath Hotel still stands, a three-storeyed building on a commanding position above the A6, between Cromford and Matlock Bath. It is easily visible, on the opposite side of the road, a little further on from Masson Mill. The 6.1 bus from Derby has a stop outside, and so from there, it is but a short walk up a path to the grounds. If arriving by car, a sloping driveway takes one straight into the car park. It is good to pause here, for across the road soar the crags of the Wild Cat Tor, – a first glimpse of the limestone gorges of Matlock Bath further North.

The Hotel is surrounded by gardens, and at the back is a large swimming pool, still fed from thermal springs. For these were the reason, both for its existence and for its name: a spring had been

The New Bath Hotel, Matlock Bath

originally discovered in 1698, a quarter of a mile further north, and the Old Bath Hotel had been erected there to accommodate visitors to it. The 'New Bath' was built in 1745, following the finding of a second warm spring .

From its beginnings in the mid-eighteenth century, then, the Hotel soon became popular, and was already mentioned in a travel guide of 1802. In 1788, its owner was Mr George Saxton, who was followed by his son

The Pavilion, Matlock Bath

William. A century later, its owner Mr Thomas Tyack, had ambitious plans for his hotel. An advertisement of that year describes its enlargement and refurbishment. There were twelve acres of grounds, adjoining those of the Old Pavilion. It could boast a billiards room, private sitting rooms, a drawing room, and five miles of fishing on the Derwent. Balls were held each week. There was a dairy farm, and, importantly in those days, 'a bus meets each train'. Many distinguished guests graced its rooms, perhaps one of the most important being the Emperor Dom Pedro II of Brazil, who stayed here with his wife in 1871.

The Hotel of today retains the elegance and grandeur of its past. The ivory and cream exterior walls are relieved by large bay windows and ornamentation. A porticoed entrance takes one into the wide hall, flanked by spacious public rooms, decorated in white and misty grey. For the hotel has been extensively refurbished, before its reopening in 2016, although it still sympathetically retains the charm of an earlier age. Inside its thick stone walls, the sounds of the A6 recede, and one can easily imagine oneself in the days when John Ruskin stayed here. The ballroom, with its chandeliers dripping from the ceiling, is now used for wedding receptions and conferences. And below the Hotel still lies the pool, fed by the original thermal spring.

Today's visitor continues south into Matlock Bath. Cafés and gift shops line one side of the road, across from the Derwent. As we walk here, we can almost imagine that we are on a promenade at the seaside! It can be busy, especially on Sundays, but it has been a holiday destination since the eighteenth century, and the atmosphere lingers. Although twenty first century tourists usually come for a few hours, rather than to stay for many days.

There is much to see along the promenade. At one end is the Pavilion, built in 1910 as a theatre and originally called the 'cure room'. The colour of its walls remind one of strawberry ice cream! It now houses a fascinating mining museum. Here too, one can gather information and leaflets. It is a good starting-point for any visit. The Pavilion was built on the site of the eighteenth century stables. In those days, carriages could be hired for visits to the great houses of Derbyshire. Donkeys, too, were waiting, to bear the tourists up the hill-sides.

Tucked among the shops across the road in North Parade are several buildings of interest. Hodgkinson's Hotel was built in the 1770s. Its name recalls its nineteenth century owner, Job Hodgkinson. The Aquarium stands where once was the thermal bath, built in 1786, and fed by water from the hillside above. Here too is the 'petrifying well', where visitors have long marvelled at the sight of objects 'turned to stone' by immersion in the mineral water. Baskets and eggs, and even wigs, were among the earlier 'souvenirs'. It remains a fascinating place to visit, with its pool and fish and photographs of old Matlock Bath.

The baths at the Hotel and Aquarium give us a clue as to the reason for the birth of Matlock Bath

Hodgkinson's Hotel, Matlock Bath

as a centre for tourism, and in fact one of the earliest. Originally, it had been a small hamlet, whose inhabitants eked out a living from farming, lead mining and quarrying. Its name is an ancient one, derived from the Old English for 'meeting place' (moot) and 'oak tree'. But the discovery of that warm water spring in 1698 would transform it forever.

A wooden, lead-lined bath was built, which could accommodate between eight and ten people. Soon the first visitors began to come to the village to bathe in and to 'take the waters'. Accommodation was needed for them, and so the development of the former village into a centre for recreation and refreshment had begun. This was at the beginning of the age when it became fashionable to treat oneself to the 'cures' offered, and also to take part in organised social gatherings. As Matlock Bath developed into a spa, no doubt the entrepreneurs hoped it would rival Bath or Tunbridge Wells! Concerts, billiards, bowls, and promenades in the pleasure gardens and into the semi-wild countryside were offered as entertainments.

In 1783, a new entrance into Matlock Bath was made at Scarthin Nick, the present day A6 crossroads at Cromford, and the bridle path from Matlock Bridge was widened. These improved the accessibility into the gorge. Hotels began to appear, among the first being the Old Bath Hotel, which had a large assembly room, as well as baths fed by the thermal spring from rocks 2000 feet above. On its site, the Royal Hotel was later built, a huge imposing building which dominated the valley and which is clearly seen on old postcards until its destruction by fire in 1929.

By the early nineteenth century then, Matlock Bath had become a well-known and fashionable spa. Its fame had spread abroad, and among its illustrious visitors were members of royal families, including the Archdukes John and Louis of Austria and the future Tsar Nicholas I. Former British Prime ministers came too, among them Sir Robert Peel (in 1835) and Earl Grey (in 1845). Queen Victoria, when still a princess, was driven from Chatsworth in 1832, and her presence certainly must have given an additional cachet to visits to the area. In the first decade and a half of that century, too, the Napoleonic Wars raged across Europe. Members of aristocratic and wealthy families who had previously travelled to the Continent, now often chose this part of Derbyshire for their 'escapes'. It was, according to Lord Byron, a 'little Switzerland', and of course much safer and more convenient of access in those turbulent years. As Mary Shelley wrote in her novel, *Frankenstein*, published in 1818, "The country, in the neighbourhood of the village resembles Switzerland, but everything is on a lower level – We visited the wondrous cave and the little cabinets of natural history." (OUP 1994 edition) No wonder that the later station was designed to remind travellers of a Swiss chalet!

For in 1849, the railways came to this corner of Derbyshire. The village at first was mainly accessible to those with the money and means to visit it. But the coming of this new form of transport would widen the popularity of the valley. The nineteenth century saw delightful residences scattered across the hillsides, many still there to admire. As well as the larger hotels, there were now thirty two lodging houses, and many refreshment rooms. Matlock Bath had become the inland seaside resort which it remains to this day!

Today's visitor has a wonderful choice of walks from Matlock Bath. One can arrive by train, or the Bakewell 'Sixes' and Transpeak buses. But one is quickly drawn away from the A6. Within minutes, one is in a quieter, more restful world. The Derwent Gardens and Lovers Walk run parallel to the Derwent. More water here, – as the gardens are fed by thermal springs!

Cross the River, and one is in ancient woodland of ash, elm, lime and yew. Take any path on the far side of the Derwent, or behind the station, and peaceful walks unravel. In late Spring, the sunlight slants through the trees. And the many-coloured mosaics of wild flowers gleam on either side of the paths.

For the natural world, perhaps surprisingly, is never far away from Matlock Bath. It was the 'wildness' which first drew the visitors here. Before the days of car and train, it would be quite an adventure to reach the dramatic, gorge-like valley. Towering limestone cliffs rise from the river. Caverns and former lead mines entice one into buried worlds. The moors are not distant. It was, on the one hand, a civilised place in which to stay – with that frisson of excitement, that remoter areas were only a walk or carriage ride away!

So, today, if one is able, climb the steep paths behind North Parade. A treasure-trail of Victorian architecture awaits. On the level walks between the ascents are attractive stone villas. One can walk in the footsteps of Queen Victoria, or visit the Temple Hotel where Lord Byron stayed and etched a poem on its window. As a reminder of the past, one can discover the 'Grotto', where the first tourists came to bathe in its spring waters. On the skyline across the valley soar the fairy-tale turrets of Riber Castle. It looks like the home of a giant, but was built in the 1860s by local magnate John Smedley, for his retirement. Derelict for many years, there are now plans for its restoration. Once completed, the apartments should certainly have many a 'room with a view'!

We can take, too, a cable car from the station. For a few thrilling moments, we hang suspended above the gorge, and gaze down at tiny cars far below. The cable car swings us to the Heights of Abraham. Pleasant hours can be spent here. We can tour the mines and caverns, learn about the ages long ago when Derbyshire was a warm lagoon or in the frozen grip of an Ice Age, and enjoy a meal at the restaurant.

It would be so easy to rush through Matlock Bath, along the A6 from Derby towards the Peak District.

But then, one would never understand the reason why so many people have been drawn to its rugged wonders.

Nor appreciate why John Ruskin delighted so much in revisiting his childhood paradise.

Matlock Bath

Engraving by Michael Vandergucht after Jeremiah Taverner 1706

8. QUARNDON –
A COUNTRY WALK WITH A MASTER SPY

Few writers can claim to have led lives more exciting and adventurous than those of their heroes.

Among them was Daniel Defoe, author of *Robinson Crusoe*.

The basic facts of his life, though, give little clue as to his achievements and complex personality. For he rose to dizzy heights – a man who counted a king and leading politicians among his friends; but one too who plunged to lowest despair as a debtor and prisoner. So, if one summarises a life as composed of birth, marriage and death, these are the facts.

Daniel Defoe was born in 1660, in the parish of Saint Giles, Cripple gate, London. He was never baptised. His father was James Foe, a butcher and tallow chandler. The family were Dissenters in their religious beliefs – that is, they were Protestants who could not conform to the rules and worship of the Church of England. James sent his son to a Dissenters' academy for his education. The beliefs and values learned as a young man would continue to influence Daniel's writings throughout his life.

In 1683, Daniel married Mary Tuffey, daughter of a wealthy cooper. They were to have eight children, six of whom survived into adulthood, – a good record for those days.

One of their homes would be in Church Street, Stoke Newington, a large house with orchards and gardens. Its size suggests a wealthy owner, as indeed he was at different periods in his life. But he died in 1731, a man on the run from his creditors, in Ropemaker Alley, Finsbury. Defoe was buried in the Protestant cemetery of Bunfield Fields. His original gravestone can now be seen in Hackney Museum.

Those, then, are the the verifiable events in his life. But, all is not quite as it seems. His father's surname was actually Foe. It was Daniel who added 'De'; and so we know him as Defoe. Perhaps it is significant that the name change happened in 1695. This was the year when he emerged from bankruptcy and was employed by the government as an accountant. He seems to have had pretensions to gentility!

He, too, appears at first sight to be a Londoner. Certainly, in all his writings, this was the city he loved and admired. It was his true home, and where his family lived.

But, travels from his youth, took him to France, Spain, the Low Countries, and possibly to Italy and Germany. He criss-crossed England, and visited Scotland several times. Defoe was a man on the move, a restless man, fascinated by places and the people he met in them.

The range of his occupations would fill many lifetimes!

He was a merchant, trading in horses, hosiery, salt, timber, wine and linen during different periods of his life. At one time, he owned a ship. At another, he established a brick works at Tilbury, and supplied bricks and tiles for Greenwich Hospital whose architect was Sir Christopher Wren.

There were rash schemes too for making a fortune. All too often, though, these would land him in prison for bankruptcy. He had dreams of investing in a diving-bell, to search for underwater treasure. A plan for involvement in the perfume industry led him to invest in a farm for breeding civet cats, from whose glands scent could be obtained. Among his steadier jobs were those of accountant and civil servant.

But it is as master spy that he would really come into his own. He set up a network of informers across the country, to gather intelligence in support of the government and his hero, the Protestant King William the Third. As R. Rowan writes,"In himself he was almost a complete secret service". He was actively influential in the events leading to the Union of England and Scotland, gathering information for English government ministers. He would be a double – agent too, as the occasion served him, perhaps at the times in his life when he needed to drag himself out of difficulties.

For Daniel Defoe courted danger. Excitement, whether in spectacular business speculation or in the shadowy world of espionage, so often seems to have been the breath of life to him. In his twenties, an idealistic young Dissenter, he supported the rebellion of the Protestant Duke of Monmouth, illegitimate son of Charles the Second, against the Catholic King James the Second. As a volunteer soldier in Monmouth's army, he would have been at the battle of Sedgemoor, when Monmouth was heavily defeated. The young Defoe fled for his life and, no doubt wisely, went abroad after the rout. He seems to have returned before or during the general pardon given by King James. His life would be one of fluctuating fortunes, with a chequered career, to say the least!

Defoe, then, was a remarkable man, who achieved the greatest fame during his lifetime. He gave support over the years to the freedom of religions and the press. Even though often at cost to himself, he defended the rights of the individual. He was a man who followed his own path despite the risks to himself and his freedom.

So, although he was a trader with a penchant for heady risk-taking, it is as a writer that he became renowned and is still remembered. He has been called the founder of British journalism. A newspaper, *The Review*, was started by him. It appeared three times weekly, and he wrote it more or less single-handed. The lead article was a vehicle developed by him to promote his views and hopefully influence those of others.

But he was master of many literary forms. In the poem, *The True-born Englishman*, he attacked the xenophobic prejudice against William of Orange, the King from Holland. Pamphlets poured from him – covering a wealth of subjects – he seemed to have an opinion on every-one and everything!

Indeed, the strength of his writing would often plunge him into hot water. Perhaps the most telling picture of Defoe is of him standing in the pillory on a charge of libel. Instead of the event being one of humiliation, he turned it into a personal triumph. By-standers could buy copies of his writings during those dramatic hours. He would even write a satirical poem, called *Hymn to the Pillory*. Ringed around by his supporters, so the story goes, he was pelted with flowers rather than with rubbish!

A Journal of the Plague Year uses a reporter's skills to create an account so realistic that he could have been there, although he was only five at the time. He has been called too, the first true novelist, works such as *Robinson Crusoe* combining imagination with vivid narrative. Defoe was a writer who could use his pen as a tool, and as a weapon, for publishing his own views. If one adds the strength of his personality and the spoken word for influencing the affairs of the country through his contacts with other people, then Defoe was indeed a formidable man.

This, then, was the Daniel Defoe who travelled through Derbyshire.

His memories, no doubt distilled from his journeys over the years, are recorded in *A Tour through the Whole Island of Great Britain*. It was published in three volumes between 1724 and1726. His Derbyshire journey is found in Volume Three, Letter Eight.

How would he have appeared to us, had we met him on his travels?

He was five foot four inches and had brown hair and grey eyes. His portrait by Jeremiah Taverner, engraved by Van der Gueht, shows him wearing a full, curly wig and cloak – a man with a high forehead, astute glance and prominent nose. There is a description of him when in London wearing a blue cloak, long wig and diamond ring. But we would probably not have taken much notice of him on many of his travels. As a secret agent, he would not have wished to draw attention to himself. So probably it was a plainly-dressed, wig-less gentleman on horseback who rode through Derbyshire.

He was clearly impressed by the county. The twelve miles between Nottingham and Derby he described as "agreeable with respect to the situation, the soil, and the well planting of the county, as any spot of ground, at least that I have seen of that length, in England." High praise indeed from such a widely-travelled man!

Derby in those days, at the birth of the Industrial Revolution, was a town "of gentry, rather than trade." He described Saint Mary's Bridge with its ancient chapel, and the Church of All Hallows, now the Cathedral, with its Cavendish monuments. It was, he wrote, "a fine, beautiful and pleasant town", with many attractive town houses in the streets around the market place. He visited the Silk Mill, and heard the story of Mr Sorocombe who fell into the river by the sluice, but miraculously was spewed out alive, thanks to the revolution of the great mill wheel.

The Derwent flowing through Derby, though, he treated with caution. "That fury of a river" was to be avoided if possible! It was, he said,"a frightful creature when the hills load her current with water." The decision was taken to ride north, and keep the river at a respectful distance.

And so he found himself in "a little ragged, but noted village", called Quarndon. Here was a famous chalybeate spring whose waters people drank and bathed in. But he was not tempted to linger. The lodgings were "wretched" in his day.

Instead, the road led him further northwards for four to five miles, until he came to higher ground. Perhaps he was pre-conditioned by travellers' tales to expect wilder countryside from here. For he described the view as "most frightful, among the black mountains of the Peak", which seems rather an exaggeration for this area!

So, he headed for Wirksworth. On the way, perhaps to his surprise, he rode through well-farmed valleys in which were prosperous markets. Part of his journey no doubt took him along the beautiful Ecclesbourne Valley, so it is perhaps no wonder that he found the route a pleasant one.

Also, evidently, the further north he went, the better the ale!

Wirksworth – or rather its inhabitants – impressed Defoe. They were lead miners, or 'Peakrills'. The town had for centuries been a centre for the industry. He was filled with compassion for them, as they spent their long working days underground. They were, he wrote, "of a strange, turbulent, quarrelsome temper", perhaps understandable in view of the dangerous lives they led. For him, the Barmoot Court was the greatest Wonder of the Peak. It had been established in the thirteenth century to settle disputes and regulate the workings of the lead mines – and still meets annually to this day.

Visitors had long been attracted to the Peak District, on whose borders Defoe now stood. Travelling to it was to experience an adventure – without having to go abroad. Stories of its wildness, its medicinal warm springs, dark caverns and great mountains lured the intrepid northwards. Many places were wrapped in mystery. So it was in a spirit of venturing into the unknown that the tourists set out for the Peak. 'Prepare to be terrified!' was probably the slogan which drew many there. On their return, their daring adventures could be recounted, to the admiration of all.

Defoe, like his contemporaries, had heard of the 'Seven Wonders of the Peak', described by writers such as Charles Cotton and the philosopher Thomas Hobbes. The 'Wonders' included Saint Anne's Well in Buxton, where Defoe bathed in the waters of the warm spring and stayed at the Old Hall Hotel; and Poole's Cavern on the outskirts of the town. The 'shivering mountain 'of Mam Tor near Castleton, and Peak Cavern in the village were two natural places to visit. In the village of Tideswell was the Ebbing and Flowing Well, although it was the Church which really impressed him. The last two were Chatsworth; and the 55 metres deep pothole, called Eldon Hole, in the Peak Forest.

Defoe was distinctly underwhelmed by them. In fact, in his scathing attack on the poetic descriptions of earlier writers, he sought to debunk the mystique which had developed around the 'Wonders'. He was the thinking man of the eighteenth century, rationalising the superstitions of the past! It is as though he delighted in his task. The inhabitants of the Peak, according to Defoe, "called everything a wonder." But they were naturally proud of their region, and wanted to share its marvels with visitors.

The Derbyshire people 200 years ago were, surely, unofficial members of a Tourist Information Office, long before tourism became a leisure industry.

And who can blame them?

Defoe did see the practical possibilities for the utilisation of Buxton's medicinal springs. From the Seven, though, only two Wonders passed his rigorous test. One of these was Chatsworth, which he described as 'a palace for a prince', and praised its architecture, grounds and setting in such a remote situation. The other was Eldon Hole, whose depth filled even Defoe with awe.

But for him, there were other wonders to be found in the area. He was engaged by Matlock Bath. Recently, one of its warm springs had been conducted into a bath house, and he enjoyed a dip in its blood-heat waters. It had potential, he thought, despite the steep, rough road to it and the lack of good accommodation. This, then, was Matlock Bath at the birth of tourism. He marvelled, too, at Matlock, or High Tor, as it is known today, rising dramatically from the Derwent as a perpendicular wall of stone on which nothing grew.

The place, though, which filled Defoe with the greatest wonder was on Brassington Moor on the way to Buxton. As he wrote, "We missed the imagined wonder and found a real one." He and his party had been advised to see 'the Giant's Tomb', but in their search, met a family who lived in a cave, perhaps the one called 'The Tomb'. The father was a lead miner, and had five children. His wife kept the cave-home clean and tidy. Two curtains divided it into three rooms where earthen ware, pewter and brass vessels were stored on shelves, and a side of bacon smoked in the chimney. Despite their poverty, the children were healthy. Outside were pigs and a cow, and a patch of barley. From his description, Defoe was clearly impressed by the family – both by the dreadful conditions in which the miner worked and the contentment of his wife. He compared their lot with that of the wealthier people he knew, and was filled with admiration and pity for them.

We leave him now, on his way northwards to Yorkshire, gathering information, fascinated by the places he visited, and most of all, delighting in the company of the people he met along the way. He has left behind for us a highly personal description of the country, its trades, villages and towns, its monuments and people – an invaluable insight into the Great Britain he loved so much.

Let us, then, return to the beginning of his tour through Derbyshire. Defoe's "ragged little settlement"of Quarndon today is an attractive village four miles from Derby. The 109 bus from Derby to Ashbourne takes one through the centre. But, this time, it is preferable to arrive by car (or on foot) from Derby, passing through the suburb of Allestree on the way. Woodlands Lane, along the ridge, passes the back of Allestree Park. On the left, there are glimpses of Kedleston Hall, with its cupola and pillared façade, especially in the winter months when the trees are leafless.

At the T-junction, where Woodlands Lane meets Burley Lane, we turn left. On the corner is a house painted black, once explained as to make it less visible from Kedleston Hall. However, the real reason is a practical one – it is painted with pitch to make it waterproof. Shortly, on the left is the Village School, and behind it, on the right, is a car park. Our walk will take us down Church Road, but first, we may wish to return to Montpelier opposite the T-junction. Here, a footpath behind the houses leads to a hill from which there is a spectacular panoramic view across the Derwent Valley. In 2001, a topograph was placed on the summit, and from its information and pictures, one can make out many places of historic interest.

But, let us return to Church Road, for our walk now begins – and a delightful one it is, in any season. To stroll down Church Road is to walk the village street, but it is one into which the countryside creeps at every turn. At its foot lie fields, giving way to gentle ridges scattered with groups of trees, and enfolding Kedleston Hall. There are glimpses of rural landscapes round every bend, but with the added fascination of history and buildings waiting to be discovered. Wooden signposts entice one to leave the road and wander across the folded fields. The stone walls of farms and enclosed gardens, of houses of warm russet brick, lure one onwards, to criss-cross the lane and unravel the story of Quarndon.

The name of the village may come from the Old English 'quern' or grinding stone; or from 'gwaum', meaning 'moor'. It has always been a farming community, and until the outbreak of the Second World War, had over twelve farms. Cattle and sheep wander its meadows. But, there were other trades and industries. One of the earliest was the manufacture of pottery. It is worth a detour on one's return to Derby to see where this was made in the thirteenth and fourteenth centuries. The site is at the bottom of Burley Hill, where it joins the A6. On the right, among the trees was the kiln, and on the left, the man-made mound which resembles a barrow was the spoil-heap for the clay. Fine examples of 'Burley Hill Pottery' can now be seen in Derby Museum. Flagons and jugs in earthy shades of green and ochre are decorated with flowers, leaves, and the horseshoes of the local de Ferrers family.

Returning to the village, behind the Joiner's Arms were once the bustling workshops of wheelwrights, blacksmiths and builders – the skilled tradesmen so necessary to any community.

Knitting was another industry. Fine silk stockings were produced on framework knitting machines in the eighteenth and nineteenth centuries. These were items to be found in the wardrobe of any fashionable gentleman in those days.

Bricks, too, were manufactured. If we spot bricks with pebbles in them in Quarndon, these are local products, hundreds of years old.

We begin our walk, then, on the left side of the road, at the Village Hall, behind which we may have parked the car. The Hall was built in 1914 by the Curzon family of Kedleston, who owned the village for part of its history. It was opened by the Revd. Albert, fourth Baron Scarsdale, father of Lord Curzon, the Foreign Secretary and Viceroy of India. The Hall is still the setting for lively Amateur Dramatic productions and concerts .

Across the road, on the corner with the Common, is a high cream-coloured stone wall. This was part of the penfold, where stray animals were kept until their owner could retrieve them, at the fine of one penny.

Next to the Village Hall stands Saint Paul's Church, built in 1874. It is the landmark of Quarndon, with its tall spire atop a tower.

Writers, though, disagree as to its appearance!

Arthur Mee recorded its "good woodwork in the pulpit and stalls, finely carved altar rails and a font of Derbyshire spar."

Nicholas Pevsner, however, was dismissive. He described the Church as "tasteless and restless, rock-faced."

As always, it is best to visit and form one's own judgement.

Outside, if one faces the spire, one can see the carved symbols of the four evangelists at its base, and the clock commemorating the Diamond Jubilee of Queen Victoria in 1897.

From 1725, there was provision for the education of the village children, and in 1859, a school was built, again thanks to Baron Scarsdale. The Headmaster's House still stands, but the other buildings were demolished in 1967 for a new school, set back from the road.

It is often by looking upwards, at the floors above street level that we can detect traces of a house's past. Number 116 was once a Methodist Chapel. The clues remain, for if we look up, we can see the triangular-shaped pediment and the words 'Wesleyan Chapel 1859' carved in stone. In its fairly short history, too, the building was used asa shop and a library, until it became a home.

As we continue down the hill, across the road we espy a white-painted building adjoining a house. It abuts the pavement and was formerly a butcher's shop. In those days, horses and carts rumbled up and down the lane. We can see the stone trough from which the weary horses drank, at Number 88.

Soon, though, ahead of us, we see the shining white walls of the pub, 'The Joiner's Arms'. The original building dates from the seventeenth century, while the adjoining brick extension was added as a Function Room in 1996. Its name recalls the history of the connections between Quarndon and the building of Kedleston Hall in the eighteenth century. This would have been a busy, noisy place for drinking and recreation for the men employed in the construction of the Hall. Nowa-days, it is open at weekends, and serves drinks and snacks at the bar.

At one time, there were five pubs in Quarndon. At least a part of the tall brick building at 93-95 was the 'William the Fourth'. Both pubs served the ale so praised by Defoe. But one wonders which one provided the "wretched lodging and entertainment"which he spurned!

There is an air of mystery to this stretch of Church Road, partly due, no doubt, to the higher banks, but also to the small stone structure next to the inn. It has the appearance of a tiny castle, with its Gothic arches and turreted top, which was roofed at one time. The door on the left led to an attendant's room, and behind was once a bath. Partly hidden by the ivy, on the back wall, is a plaque recording the visit of Daniel Defoe.

For this was the site of the famous chalybeate spring, which once flowed through the lion's mouth. From at least as early as the

The Joiner's Arms, Quarndon

seventeenth century, the spring with its iron content was visited for its healing properties. We can, perhaps, imagine the many people who travelled here in search of a cure for theirdistressing conditions. Among the claims made for its uses weretreatments for 'fluxes', aches, colic, fevers, anaemia and asthma. No wonder it became popular to drink the water and bathe in it. In the days of Oliver Cromwell, there was the added 'attraction' of two to three hour long sermons on Sunday afternoons, delivered from its rooftop!

No waters, healing or otherwise, now flow through the lion's mouth. A series of earth tremors from 1863 to 1956 gradually stopped the spring. And any dream of developing Quarndon into an eighteenth century Bath were lost in the mists of the past.

Once though, this quiet lane must have been a busy thoroughfare. Across the road, at 53-57, a pathway leads past the cottages into Battelles Lane, and so to Kedleston Road. This was the old route from Derby to Manchester. Instead of walkers peacefully wandering the track, stage coaches rushed passengers through Quarndon. One wonders how their speeds compared with those of the cars of today?

In fact, if one was driving down Church Road, one would miss one of its oldest buildings all together! For almost at the end of the road,

The chalybeate spring in Quarndon

where the meadows and parkland of Kedleston lie so near, is Old Vicarage Lane. This was probably the centre of the original village. In the field where two steams meet at the bottom of the Lane once stood the mill. It dated from the twelfth century, but probably fell into disuse after the Black Death of 1348-51, when the population of the country shrunk by a third.

The Hall with its farm stood nearby, although the Hall was demolished in 1812.

Lion's mouth, chalybeate spring

But there is a tantalising 'ghost' of that long lost village. It lies up the sloping path between the houses above Old Vicarage Lane. At first glance, it appears to be a tree wrapped in ivy. But, if we venture closer, we can see that the ivy stems twist among the stones of a tower. In fact, it is difficult to see where plant ceases and wall begins, the two are so closely entwined with each other. This is all that remains of the original twelfth century Church, demolished in 1874 when the centre of Quarndon moved up the hill. Old photographs and engravings show it to have had a short West tower, topped by a four-sided spire. There was a Norman doorway, a stone altar and a musicians' gallery. The memorial stones are still to be found, though, lying flat in the churchyard around the tower. It is perhaps a good place, this 'country churchyard', in which to pause and reflect a while on the generations

of people who have lived in this charming village. How many changes have been witnessed in those thousand years!

For now our walk retraces our steps. We can see the houses on our return from different angles, and discover all that we might have missed in our descent. Reunited with the car, we can take the road, called The Common, straight ahead. In Springtime, it is a delight to drive along it. Daffodils rim the road in golden streams. From Quarndon, we can proceed to the crossroads, and turn left. A pleasant afternoon, with a stroll in Kedleston Park, a visit to the Hall, and tea and cake in its former kitchen will then complete our day in Quarndon.

Kedleston Hall

John Wesley by George Romney (1789)
Courtesy of The New Room, John Wesley's Chapel in Bristol

9. RAMBLING AROUND ROWSLEY

The earlier travellers to Derbyshire, in the eighteenth and nineteenth centuries, often stayed in one place, using it as a base from which to venture further afield. Castleton, for example, would be a village in which to find safety and shelter, on the very edge of wilder countryside, of nearby caves and further moors. From Bakewell, Chatsworth and other great houses would tempt the visitor from town to parkland and palatial architecture. Horses, carriages, stagecoaches, and later, railways and buses, would ease the journey. From these, the more energetic and adventurous visitors could then take the footpaths to the hills and along the valleys.

Matlock Bath has long been ideal as a venue in itself for holidays, and with a variety of accommodation to be found in its hotels and villas. But it has always been popular too, as the starting point for excursions.

Sometimes, it is good to leave a place for a while during one's visit, to stand back, and then to return to it. For often, such a comparison can enable one to appreciate its charms even more. So perhaps we too can follow in the footsteps of those earlier visitors to the area, and travel further northwards for a few hours, or even for a day.

Nowadays, the journey is made easier for us than it would have been in the past. The 6.1 and Transpeak buses take us smoothly along the A6.

In minutes, we arrive at the bustling town of Matlock itself, where echoes of its Victorian heritage are still evident in its sturdy stone rows of shops, attractive Hall Leys Gardens, and in the huge Hydro, built by John Smedley in 1853, and which dominates the town to this day.

The Derwent will draw us to follow its course towards Chatsworth. But for our trip from Matlock Bath, we will pause where the Wye flows into it. At the confluence of the two rivers lies the village of Rowsley. Its tranquil setting in an open valley is a good foil to the cliffs of the place we have left. Although the A6 certainly passes through it on its way to Bakewell, we soon can find ourselves on winding paths between the conical hills crowned with groups of trees, and the noise of the traffic dies away. In Winter, the hills here turn white more quickly than further downstream. The snow lingers too in gulleys and shadows, leaving behind it, zebra-striped slopes. Early Spring is a special time, before the crowds descend on this part of the Derwent Valley. Grey-gauze mists veil and soften the skyline. The first shimmer of green speaks of Summer days ahead. Soon daffodils gild the village lawns and line the lanes, and sheep dot the hillsides like limestone boulders.

In the centre, then, of this corner of Derbyshire is Rowsley, and at its heart, proudly stands the Peacock Hotel. Above its porch is a carved peacock, part of the crest of the Manners family. The Hotel was originally built as a house in 1652 by John Stevenson, the agent of Lady Manners. It was once the Dower House to nearby Haddon Hall, whose turrets and terraces tower half hidden behind trees and copper beech hedges – like some Sleeping Beauty's castle. The Peacock in its long history became an inn and a farmhouse, and is now an attractive hotel furnished with antiques and interesting old paintings. It is a delightful place in which to have coffee or a meal, or in which to stay while visiting the Peak District. One is in good company, for among its guests have been the American poet Henry Longfellow and the artist Sir Edwin Landseer.

The Peacock Hotel, Rowsley
© The Peacock Hotel

Rowsley, even though in itself a small village, is actually composed of two hamlets, – Great Rowsley on the West bank of the Derwent and Little Rowsley on the East bank.

Little Rowsley was sparsely populated until the coming of the railway in 1849. A new station was opened in 1862, – advertised as 'Rowsley for Chatsworth'. Many distinguished visitors alighted at the station on their way to Chatsworth. The elegant first-class waiting room is certainly an echo of its past use. A subway was built, too, in 1891, no doubt to protect august travellers from the weather of Derbyshire! It closed in 1967, although marshalling yards and railway buildings have nowadays enjoyed a second lease of life as a designer village. In the 1880s, many houses were built, including 'Midland Cottages', originally occupied by railway employees and their families. Both the first station and the Cottages were designed by Sir Joseph Paxton, architect of the Crystal Palace.

Great Rowsley was much older and was an Anglo Saxon settlement. Its name 'Reuslege' means 'clearing in a forest'. The local stone houses we see today, however, are from much later dates, being mostly from the eighteenth and nineteenth centuries. Among the most splendid are

The entrance of the Peacock Hotel, Rowsley
Tom Kahler © The Peacock Hotel

The bar in the Peacock Hotel, Rowsley
Tom Kahler © The Peacock Hotel

'Holly House' and 'The Beeches', built in 1710, as one residence, as the Manor House. This was once the home of the botanist Sir Francis Darwin, the third son of Charles Darwin.

A walk up the lane to the left of the Peacock brings one to the Norman-style Church of Saint Katherine, erected in 1855. From here, there are views across the Wye Valley. We can perhaps pause and reflect on the changes this quiet place has seen in its history. That story is interwoven with that of the Manners family, which owned the village and provided houses and employment. The Church. School, Village Hall and Recreation Field were all made possible through them. According to the 1841 census, a blacksmith, wheelwright, shoemakers, sawyer and joiner were to be found at Rowsley. Until 1947, ten farms still worked the land around the village. The coming of the railway certainly of course contributed to the transformation of Rowsley. Its trains hurried milk from the farms to London, as well as tourists from London to the Peak.

In the days of the railways, there was often excitement at Rowsley. Members of the royal family and many illustrious members of society used Rowsley Station when staying with the Dukes of Devonshire at

Home Farm, Rowsley

Chatsworth. King Edward VII and Queen Alexandra were regular visitors, especially at New Year. The King and Queen of Portugal came by train in 1904. A final royal visit by royal train took place in 1933, when King George V and Queen Mary came to stay with the Devonshires. Peaceful Rowsley must have been awakened to drama and bustle and colour with these comings and goings of the 'great and the good' of the land, on their way to Chatsworth!

Long before the railways, however, in 1788, another distinguished visitor came that way. An elderly John Wesley, founder of the Methodist Church, and by that time, long famed across the country for his preaching and writing, was travelling to Derby. He was then aged 85, dressed neatly in black, with silver white hair under a tri-corn hat. His journeys had already taken him the length and breadth of the country, as well as to the States, Germany and the Netherlands.

Wesley was born in 1703, the son of the Reverend Samuel Wesley, Rector of Epworth, Lincolnshire, and his wife Susanna. John was their

John Wesley by John Michael Williams
(1710-c1780)
By kind permission of Lincoln College, University of Oxford, photographed by Keith Barnes

fifteenth child. One significant event from his childhood years was always remembered by the family. In 1709, when he was only six, a fire broke out in the Rectory. John was trapped upstairs and was rescued only shortly before the house was destroyed. The family was convinced that he had been rescued for a special purpose, as, "a brand plucked from the burning."

John Wesley was educated at Charterhouse School, London and Christ Church Oxford. In 1726, he was elected Fellow of Lincoln College Oxford. Two years later, he was ordained priest in the Church of England, and, as well as preaching, became recognised as a conscientious tutor. At Oxford, a group led by, among others John's brother Charles, the future great hymn writer, had been formed. Their purpose was to meet together for Bible study, prayer and the pursuit of a devout Christian life. But they also sought to put their faith into practice, visiting prisons, taking food to the poor and teaching orphans to read. They became known as 'The Holy Club'. John joined the group in 1729, and soon became its leader, with the meetings held in his rooms at Lincoln College. Critics of the disciplined life style of the members, soon nicknamed them 'Methodists', a name which would one day be given to those who belonged to the Methodist Church.

A strong sense of vocation to share the Christian faith overseas led Wesley to leave Oxford in 1735, to spend two years in Georgia, in the United States. There, he was Chaplain to the Colony, and ministered to both the settlers and the indigenous population.

His adventurous travels too were already beginning – with treks into the undeveloped countryside, down the coast from Savannah, often sleeping in the open, and living on bear meat. Here as well, he made a first collection of Hymns and Psalms, which became the first Anglican Hymnal in the United States. But it was not to be all success and achievement, and after a troubled romance which ended with the lady's marriage to another man, Wesley decided to leave Georgia.

On his return to London, and searching for new direction in his life, he went, in May 1738, to a meeting at Aldersgate Street. As he wrote, "About a quarter before nine, while (the preacher) was describing the change which God works in the heart through faith in Christ, I felt my heart strangely warmed". This, often described as his 'evangelical conversion', would be the great turning point in his life. From then onwards, he felt the call to preach the Gospel wherever he went, not only in churches, but in fields, to those who worked in the mills and mines, in market places and in homes, – wherever people gathered to listen. As he said, "The world is my parish."

Wesley travelled 250,000 miles, on foot or horseback, and in his later years in carriages. From Northern Scotland to the Channel Islands, from Wales to Ireland, many places still preserve the memory that, 'John Wesley preached here.' Among the towns and villages of Derbyshire which Wesley visited are Ashbourne, Bakewell, Bolsover, Bongs, Buxton (where he conducted a wedding at St. Ann's Church travelling from Derby in a post-chaise and bringing the bride with him!), Chapel-en-le-Frith, Chesterfield, Chinley, Crich, Hayfield, New Mills and Ockbrook.

In Derby, an unruly crowd's response to his preaching in the Market Place forced him to withdraw for his own safety to the home of the Dobinsons in Iron Gate. But by 1765, he could lead a service in a Methodist Chapel in St. Michael's Lane, near the Cathedral.

Wesley was a powerful, effective preacher, with a message of hope and personal salvation, whose words and example transformed the lives of countless men and women, and eventually led to the great religious revival and the foundation of the worldwide Methodist Church. Regular worship, meeting for fellowship, evangelism, and practical caring service for others would be among its hallmarks. As Wesley wrote, "Do all the good you can, by all the means you can, in all the ways you can, in all the places you can, at all the times you can, to all the people you can, as long as ever you can."

Today, Methodist churches and chapels are to be found in thousands of communities across the world.

However, a visit to one of three places sheds particular light on Wesley's life. The Old Rectory at Epworth is open to the public and gives glimpses of family life in the Eighteenth Century, as well as possessing a delightful physic garden. At Bristol, where he first preached outdoors, is The New Room (or John Wesley's Chapel), where the first Methodist building in the world can be visited. Charles Wesley's House is next door. In London, Wesley's Chapel, City Road includes both place of worship and museum. In the small graveyard behind the Chapel lies his grave .

John Wesley published many works, including his *Forty four Sermons and Notes to the New Testament*. But for insight into his personality, and into the thrilling events of his travels, reading his Journal is a 'must'. It is here that we learn of his visit to Rowsley.

As he wrote in his entry for 11TH July 1788, "We set out early for Derby. About 9, within about a mile of the Peacock, suddenly the axle tree of my chaise snapped asunder, and the carriage overturned." The horses, thankfully, stood still, "while we crept out of the fore-windows. The broken glass cut one of my gloves a little, but did us no other damage."

He no doubt received warm Derbyshire hospitality, probably at the Peacock itself, before resuming his travels. That same evening, he preached in Derby, and was up early next day, to speak again at 5am!

Today though, as we go back to the crossroads at the Peacock, we gaze down the Valley and enjoy timeless and tranquil scenes. We return to the A6 and cross over the road, to visit one of the other fascinating buildings of Rowsley. This is Caudewell's Mill. There was a mill here certainly as far back as the Middle Ages – the earliest record of it being 1339, in the Receipt Rolls of the Dean and Chapter of Lichfield. The site near the junction of the two rivers provided power and so, at different times in its history, there have been a corn mill, a walk mill for fulling cloth and a saw mill. These buildings were demolished in 1874 by John Caudwell, to build the mill we see today. It was in use successfully until 1978. Today, it is run by Caudewell's Mill Trust Ltd., and is a fascinating site to visit. There are displays and hands-on models where one can learn about how wheat is turned into flour. A stroll along the head race nature trail gives glimpses of the Wye Valley, and a vegetarian café is an attractive place from which to see the River over lunch, – providing a fitting conclusion to a 'day out' in Rowsley!

The visit, then, to this timeless place provides an effective contrast to

the wonders of the gorges of Matlock Bath. As we return to one of its hotels, to enjoy its amenities and to think about its dramatic landscape after the excursion to a gentler part of the county, perhaps those hours away have allowed us to appreciate it even more.

Caudewell's Mill, Rowsley

George Eliot (Mary Ann Cross née Evans)
Replica by Francois D'Albert Durade 1849, National Portrait Gallery 1405
By kind permission of the National Portrait Gallery

Visiting Wirksworth and seeing its houses is like turning the pages of a book of architecture. Some line the streets in terraces. Others resemble small manor houses, and were once the homes of wealthy lead mine owners. One of the houses just outside the Close, in Coldwell Street, was once the home of Sir Frederick Treves, who left Wirksworth to become a distinguished Royal Surgeon and Professor of Medicine. Among his patients were Edward VII and Joseph Merrick, the so-called 'Elephant Man', whom he befriended.

In September, during theArts Festival, it is possible to look inside many of the houses, when their owners open their doors to visitors, in order to show the work of local artists. There are refreshments at many venues, an architectural and arts trail to enjoy and a variety of performances – all bringing the streets of Wirksworth to colourful life.

For over the centuries, Wirksworth has been the centre of many industries. It was not always as peaceful as it seems today.

Lead mining took place around it at least as early as Roman times, and was carried out extensively in the days of the Saxons. According to the Domesday Book, Wirksworth possessed a church with a priest, – and three lead mines.

There is an amazing reminder of the legacy of the lead mining industry in Chapel Street. It is a solid-looking Georgian stone building, with two large windows flanking a stepped entrance. On either side of the doorway are marble plaques depicting miners' scales, picks and trays. They are a clue to its purpose. For this is the Moot Hall, builtin 1874 to house the Bar Mote Court. The earliest reference to the Court is in 1288, but its origins are probably earlier. In fact, it is believed to be the earliest industrial court in the country, possibly in the world! In the Court, lead was measured, in special scales dating from the reign of Henry VIII, disputes were settled and taxes collected. Wirksworth for centuries had been the centre of an area of 115 square miles, known as the Kings Field, an area in which anyone could search for lead ore, except in churchyards, orchards and highways. So it made sense, for practical purposes, to hold a regular meeting in the town, to regulate the industry. An earlier Moot Hall, built in 1773, once stood in the Market Place, but was demolished because of the rowdy behaviour of the miners! The Bar Mote Court, though, still meets once a year in Chapel Street. Among its ancient customs is the provision of bread, cheese and clay pipes, a reminder of the lingering traditions from Wirksworth's distinguished past.

Limestone quarries flourished too, – their great bites gouged into the hillsides still visible today. The stone was taken down the Ecclesbourne Railway to the main line, and so to all parts of the country.

Cotton and silk mills once contributed to its prosperity, and remain to this day.

Haarlem Mill, built by Richard Arkwright in 1780, is the still impressive building on the left as one enters from the Derby road, although now some of it is in dereliction. It was the first cotton mill to use a steam engine. The building which at one time housed Wirksworth Heritage Centre, was a silk mill in the past. In them, red tape was manufactured – a thin line woven from Wirksworth to Westminster!

In the early part of the nineteenth century, one of the mill managers was a man called Samuel Evans. He and his wife Elizabeth lived in Wirksworth for many years, where they were both Methodist local preachers. Their niece was Mary Anne Evans, better known as the writer George Eliot.

Over the years , several visits are recorded between niece and uncle and aunt. George Eliot stayed with them in Wirksworth in 1826 and 1840. In 1839 and 1842, Mr and Mrs Evans visited their niece.

The woman who walked the narrow streets of Wirksworth in her youth would become one of the greatest writers in English literature. But her life would also be one of many contrasts and contradictions. Born into a comfortable background in the heart of a fertile farming landscape, she would also in her childhood have seen miners leaving their homes to work in the pits. Her beliefs would change from those of an evangelical Christian to those of a free-thinking radical. She would flout convention by living with a married man, and later by marrying a man over twenty years her junior. As a single woman working as a journalist, she would be unusual in the Victorian world of the 1850s. Yet her abilities were recognised early by her contemporaries such as Dickens and Queen Victoria, who commissioned two paintings of scenes from *Adam Bede*, the story of an unmarried mother sentenced for the killing of her baby.

Famous today as George Eliot, the visitor to her Aunt Elizabeth in Wirksworth called herself by four other names as well. She was named Mary Anne Evans at birth, but from 1837 called herself Mary Ann

Evans. From 1851, she was 'Marian', and from 1854 was Marian Evans Lewes. Finally, after her marriage in 1880, she was known as MaryAnn Cross.

Mary Anne Evans was born, then, on 22 November 1819 at South Farm, Arbury, near Nuneaton, Warwickshire, to Robert Evans and his second wife Christiana. Robert was the manager of large estates belonging to the Newdigate family, who lived at Arbury Hall. A well-respected man, he not only managed the estates, but was a skilled craftsman and carpenter. After 1820, the family moved to Griff House, a large farm on the estate, which he also ran. It is believed that many of his admirable traits are reflected in the personality of his daughter's hero, Adam Bede, like him, a trusted and talented craftsman. Griff House, a rambling, well-run farmhouse surrounded by lush green countryside, was Mary Anne's home for twenty years. It was during those early years, too, that she visited her father's relations in Derbyshire and Staffordshire, including the Evanses in Wirksworth.

Robert Evans arranged a good education for his children. Mary Anne attended various local schools, and then boarded at Nuneaton and Coventry. In 1835, though, she returned home to help her family. Her mother had become ill, and died the next year. So, for the next few years, Mary Anne was housekeeper for her father and brother Isaac. She had excelled in English and French at school, and was a talented pianist. Her father recognised the fact that he had a gifted daughter, and so invited teachers to their home, where she could continue her language and music lessons.

In 1841, however, her brother Isaac married, and Robert decided to retire. He and his daughter moved to a comfortable house in Coventry. There she was to meet the family who would bring about the changes which would affect the rest of her life. For their neighbours had a brother called Charles Bray, married to Cara. The Brays' home was a meeting-place for radical thinkers, and Mary Anne was drawn into their circle, one in which she soon became a lively, leading conversationalist. During this time too, she was engaged in translating *The Life of Jesus* by the radical thinker D.F. Strauss from the German, completing the work in 1846.

When her father died in 1849, the Brays invited her to accompany them on a six week tour of the Continent. They returned home, but Mary Anne stayed in Geneva over the Winter, lodging with the artist François D'Albert Durade and his wife. It is from this visit that we have the most famous portrait of the future novelist. She leans towards us, with the beginnings of a smile, her head slightly tilted as though she is about to speak. Her light brown hair is thick, and parted in the centre. Blue eyes sparkle with animation.

This is perhaps the most flattering of the portraits, compared with others depicting her, for she was not a conventional beauty according to the tastes of the age in which she lived. Several other portraits survive. Mrs Cara Bray painted her friend in watercolours in 1842. There are chalk and pencil drawings by F. W. Burton executed in 1864 and 1865. Lady Alma Tadema produced two pencil profiles in 1877; while Samuel Lawrence drew the writer in 1860. There is even a photograph of a pensive 'George Eliot', taken in 1858.

They all seem less flattering, more true to life perhaps than the Durade portrait, which is the one usually reproduced in biographies of the novelist. They certainly echo the written descriptions which come down to us. These portraits show her with thick, darker brown hair, grey eyes, a predominant nose and long jaw. In most, though, as in the Durade picture, her head is tilted slightly forward, with a look of enquiry and lively interest. One can well imagine her holding the listener's attention as she engaged him in conversation. Indeed, the writer Henry James, although not at first drawn to her physical appearance, wrote to his father in 1869, "In her ugliness resides a most powerful beauty which, in a very few minutes steals forth and charms the mind, so that you end, as I ended, in falling in love with her".

From Geneva, then, Mary Anne returned to Coventry, and to the home of the Brays, where she spent much of her time in translating and in writing articles .

Already, she was displaying the independent nature, which was to develop over the years. In 1851, she took the courageous step for a single woman at that time by going to London to work as a journalist. She lodged with the publisher John Chapman and his family. Chapman owned the periodical, *The Westminster Review*, and asked Mary Anne to be its editor.

At the Chapman's house in the Strand, and through her own articles and authorship, she now began to move among the most eminent writers of the day. Charles Dickens, Robert Browning, Thomas Carlyle, and William Gladstone were among the distinguished men whom she met at this time. To the Strand, too, came the philosopher Herbert Spencer, with whom a close friendship developed. For Mary Anne, this deepened into love, but one which was to remain unrequited, as Spencer did not share her feelings.

Although Mary Anne was deeply hurt by his rejectionof her, it was with one of his friends that she was to find happiness. In 1851, she met the scientific writer and philosopher, George Henry Lewes. He became a regular contributor to the Review, and by1853, they had become inseparable companions. Lewes was married with three children. But the marriage was an unhappy one, and Lewes was unwilling to divorce his wife, as he had acknowledged one of her children by another man as his own. He and Mary Anne fell in love, and from October 1853, they began to live together, calling themselves 'Mr and Mrs Lewes'. Theirs was to be a happy, fulfilled relationship until his death in 1878. In July 1854, because of the scandal caused by the fact that they were living together, they travelled to Germany, where they stayed until March 1855. During their time there, Mary Anne worked on the translation of Baruch Spinoza's *Ethics* from the German, which would be completed in 1856. Eventually, they settled in Richmond, Surrey, although their travels continued over the years.

It was Lewes who encouraged her to begin to write stories. So, from her articles and reviews, she turned to fiction. The first work to be published, by John Blackwood in 1857, was called *Scenes of Clerical Life*, and was set in a fictional 'Milby', really Nuneaton.

The 'Scenes' were followed by her first full-length novel, *Adam Bede*, published in 1859. In order to preserve her anonymity, as she was living with a married man, she called herself 'George Eliot'. 'George' was after Lewes, and 'Eliot' was chosen as it was 'a good mouth-filling, easily pronounced word'. Authors would also be more accepted as serious writers in Victorian times if they were men rather than women, and for Mary Anne, realism in story-telling was essential.

Other novels followed, penetrating studies of human nature, such as *Silas Marner, Romola, The Mill on the Floss, Middlemarch, Felix Holt*, and *Daniel Deronda*. They would be numbered among the classics of English literature.

When Lewes died, Mary Anne was plunged into despair, through the loss of the man whom she loved so deeply. Among the few people who would bring her some consolation was John Walter Cross. He was a retired banker, a bachelor of forty when he met the Leweses. His mother had died a few days after Mary Anne had lost Lewes. Their shared grief seems to have drawn them together, for although he was twenty years her junior, they were married in 1880.

Theirs was to be a brief marriage. After a honeymoon tour which included a stay in Venice, they returned to London and moved to a large house at 4, Cheyne Walk. On 18 December, they attended a concert. Mary Anne caught a chill. Within four days, she was dead. She was buried in unconsecrated ground near to the grave of George Lewes, in Highgate Cemetery, London.

Hers had been an unconventional life. She was a highly-educated and intelligent woman, with a searching and questioning mind. At the same time, she was capable of strong emotional feelings. These different traits in her personality combined to form a remarkable and unique writer. Her novels are masterpieces of insight into human psychology. They are written with compassion and sympathy for her characters, including those deemed social outcasts in the age in which she lived. The countryside and towns of her formative years certainly provided the settings for her novels They live in the descriptions she paints of them, so clearly in fact, that one can imagine oneself walking their lanes and fields in her company. But the novels transcend them too. For the personalities of her characters live and breathe in such a compelling way, that they could be those found inany age or place.

It is perhaps, then, fitting that the story she first heard in her youth, in Wirksworth, the story of an unmarried girl who murdered her baby, is the one which evolved into her first novel, *Adam Bede*.

On one of her visits to Wirksworth, George Eliot had heard the poignant tale which was to play such a moving part in her novel. Her Aunt Elizabeth Evans used to visit Nottingham prison. There, she had met a young girl convicted of murdering her child. Elizabeth talked and prayed with her. She went with her to the place of execution, and did what she could on the way, to bring some comfort to her.

That story, dramatically-told, appears in chapters 41 – 43 of the novel. Here, the heroine Dinah Morris visits the pitiful Hetty Sorrel in prison. Hetty has been found guilty of killing her baby, and faces execution. On the way, Dinah rides with her in the cart, to offer her support. In real life, the journey ended in execution. In the novel, Arthur Donnithorne, Hetty's lover and the father of her child, appears on horseback with a last-minute reprieve.

After *Adam Bede* had been published in 1859, George Eliot described how her Aunt's memory had provided the story at its heart – fact and fiction; Elizabeth Evans and the heroine Dinah Morris.

But are there any other connections between them?

Their appearance was certainly different. Elizabeth is described by her niece as 'a tiny woman with bright small dark eyes and black hair' and as being 'naturally excitable". The heroine Dinah had pale, reddish hair, mild grey eyes and a calm dignified manner.

And yet, both were Methodist local preachers. Elizabeth, like Dinah, had a strong reputation as a visiting evangelist. Both travelled to cities away from their homes for their work, – Elizabeth to Nottingham, and Dinah to Leeds.

The novelist weaves together pictures of the Derbyshire and Staffordshire which she knew so well, with the places of her imagination.

George Eliot's Aunt Elizabeth Evans, preaching in later years

So Staffordshire becomes 'Loam shire'; Derbyshire, 'Stony shire'.

Derby is 'Stoniton'; Ashbourne, 'Oakbourne'.

The village of 'Hayslope', the home of Adam Bede and the setting for much of the narrative, is Ellastone in Staffs.

While 'Snowfield', where Dinah lives, is Wirksworth.

There are two clear descriptions of the town. But each is coloured by the hero's mood .

His first visit to Snowfield, to find Dinah, is influenced by his despair. To him, Wirksworth appears "grim,stony, and unsheltered,up the side of a steep hill". (chapter 35).

But the second is more positive and hopeful, as Adam has discovered his love for Dinah. The landscape, like his mood, takes on new possibilities as he rides towards the town where she lives. "The scene looked less harsh in the soft October sunshine than it had done in the eager time of early spring; and the one grand charm it possessed in

common with all wide – stretching wood less regions – that it filled you with a new consciousness of the over-arching sky – had a milder, more soothing influence than usual, on this almost cloudless day." (chapter 48)

The "grey town", the "ugly red mill" are still there for Adam, but transformed into something beautiful through his feelings.

In each, features – such as the Ecclesbourne stream, the mill, the steep hill up which the streets climb, the wide horizons – are easily recognisable to this day.

Others remain too. A solidly-built stone house with large windows has long been called 'Adam Bede Cottage'. Nowadays, its roof is of slate, but older pictures show it once was thatched. It stands at right-angles to the road from Derby, opposite Haarlem Mill. Samuel and Elizabeth Evans came to live here in 1814. So, it would have been in this house that their niece came to stay in 1826.

Did her memories later transform it into the home of her heroine, Dinah? For it too was thatched, outside the town, sideways to the road, and near the mill.

Fact and fiction, woven together in the homes of the heroines Elizabeth and Dinah?

The copper beech tree marking the burial place of Elizabeth Evans

In King Street, there is a blue plaque on the wall of the grocer's shop. For this is the house where Elizabeth Evans lived in her later years.

She was buried in an unmarked grave in Wirksworth Churchyard.

Adam Bede's Cottage,
where George Eliot came to stay in 1826

Above it grows a stately copper beech. The memorial tablet recording the deaths of Elizabeth in 1849, and of Samuel in 1858, is at the time of writing in the Heritage Centre.

Surely though, no finer memorial to Elizabeth Evans – her strong, lively faith and compassionate nature – can be found than in her niece's portrayal of Dinah Morris in her novel, *Adam Bede*.

THE JOURNEY CONTINUES

Derbyshire is a county made for discovery.

Motorways soon lead the visitor to quieter roads. Roads give way to lanes, which in their turn, narrow to footpaths, tracing a valley or climbing to the horizon.

The paths themselves will entice the rambler into the hills of the Peak, to higher skylines and wilder spaces. A stile takes the path into another field, a further meadow. A gate opens into a wood, enclosing the walker in a different world of overarching trees and shaded avenues. Stone walls across a hillside radiate from a farm at their heart;

From the series of books, 'The Beauties of England and Wales' engraving of Derby
from a drawing by H. Moore/James Greig c1805

and ancient circles journey into the past, reminders of the long-forgotten people who once worshipped there.

Derbyshire, it is true, is a long way from the sea, being in the East Midlands. But rivers, lakes and reservoirs reflect its skies. One of its rivers, the Derwent, is now a heritage corridor, as a birthplace of the Industrial Revolution. To travel along its length, from Derby northwards, is to be reminded of its importance in the History of not only England, but of the world. The mills are still there, in places such as Derby, Milford, Belper and Cromford, and offer fascinating insights into that past.

The great treasure houses of the county invite one to step through their doors into a more elegant age. As well as their paintings and furnishings, though, they provide a glimpse into the lives of those who built the houses and collected the objects. Here too, the visitor can walk the landscape, tamed and transformed into parkland and gardens, following in the footsteps of Elizabeth Bennett at Pemberley.

Across the county are the villages, many built out of the local rock and so perfectly blending into the countryside. Many are very ancient and betray their origins in their names, from Old English, Scandinavian, or Norman French. Some, such as Elvaston (Aelfwald's tun or settlement) or Muggington (the settlement of Muca's folk) are reminders of landowners. Others, such as Belper (beautiful retreat) or Hartshorne (hart's bend) reveal no doubt areas in which deer were once hunted. Some are simply descriptive of the places themselves – Ley (clearing), Heage (ridge), Hope (valley) or Crich (hill).

For some of the villages, the passing years have led to prosperity and growth, transforming them into market towns, like Bakewwell or Wirksworth. Many contain churches and houses, centuries old, and well worth a visit.

The county city of Derby is gateway to the Derwent Valley World Heritage Site. Mills beside the River speak of its industrial past. The mediaeval Bridge Chapel tells of the dangers of travelling in those days. For here, people would pause and pray before the next stage of their journey. Streets such as Friargate, Sadlergate and Iron Gate rival those to be found in any historic city. In Iron Gate stands the Cathedral, a bright and elegant place of worship, through whose glass doors and windows the light streams through to the East End. From the tower, a panoramic view across the city unfolds, while inside are the splendours of the monument to the formidable Grande Dame, Bess of Hardwick. At the end of Sadlergate are the Art Gallery and Museum, which house a collection of treasures, – from a Bronze Age canoe to the paintings of Joseph Wright.

Roads from Derby though, draw one into the countryside, and so to the Peak District. For the county is to be enjoyed at any time of the year. In the spring, lambs decorate the hills, and daffodils brighten many a village green. Summer brings people to enjoy the peace of the parks or the bustle of Bakewell. Autumn transforms the moors to rich purple and bronze; and Winter snows bleach the peaks into a dazzling world of long views and clear skies.

The journey of discovery, then, can continue, whether to places, through the countryside, or into the past. This book includes those towns and villages where one can still find traces of writers who visited the area, in sites open to the public. But in any journey, there is always more to explore and this is true for the authors too. Florence Nightingale found peace here after the Crimea in her home at Lea; the philosopher Thomas Hobbes once walked the corridors of Old Hardwick, as tutor to the young Cavendishes; and Isaac Walton and Charles Cotton, those 'compleat anglers', fished the waters of the Dove.

For the visitor to Derbyshire, the travelling – and the adventure – continue.

The Old House Museum, Bakewell

BIBLIOGRAPHY

Adams, Kathleen: *George Eliot* (Pitkin Guides 2002)

Austen, Jane: *Pride and Prejudice* (first published 1813.
    Penguin Classics 1996)

Barker, Juliet: *The Brontes* (Phoenix Classics 1994)

Bayles, Freda and Ede, Janet: *Alison Uttley's Country Walks*
    (Darrand, Matlock Bath,1995)

Bayles, Freda and Ede, Janet: *The Cromford Guide*
    (Scarthin 1994, revised 2001)

Blunt, A.W.F. (ed.): *The See of Derby, being a Souvenir for the Foundation
    of new Diocese of Derby* (Bemrose, Derby)

Bronte, Charlotte: *Jane Eyre* (first published 1847. Pan Books 1967)

Caudewell's Mill Trust Ltd., information leaflets

Clarke, Liam: *Castleton. A History* (Amberley Publishing 2014)

Clarke, Liam: Castleton. *A History, a Tour, People, Buildings and
    Industries* (Owl, 2009)

Craven, Maxwell: *Derbeians of Distinction* (Breedon, Derby 1998)

Davison, A.W.: *Derby: its rise and progress* (Bemrose Derby 1906)

Defoe, Daniel: *A Tour through the whole Island of Great Britain*
    (1724, Penguin 1971, reprinted in Penguin Classics 1986,
    edited by Pat Rogers)

Dixon Hurst, John: *The Wider Sea. A Life of John Ruskin* (J.M Dent 1982)

Drabble, Margaret (ed.),: *Oxford Companion to English Literature.*
    New Edition (OUP 1985)

Eliot, George: *Adam Bede* (Collins, first published 1859,
    reprinted 1973, editor: G.F. Mains)

Emmans, Les: *Erasmus Darwin. Derby's Forgotten Genius*
    (Lindens Music , 2010)

Haight, Gordon S.: *George Eliot. A Biography* (OUP 1968)

Harman, Claire: *Charlotte Bronte. A Life* (first published by
    Viking 2015, published in Penguin Books 2016)

Hilton, Tim: *John Ruskin, The Early Years* (Yale 1985)

Jackson, Kevin: *The Worlds of John Ruskin* (The Ruskin Foundation)

Jackson Bate, W.: *Samuel Johnson* (Counterpoint 1998)

Johnson, Edgar: *Sir Walter Scott. The Great Unknown*
    (Macmillan, 1970)

King-Hele, Desmond: *Erasmus Darwin. A Life of unequalled achievement*
    (Giles de la Mere Publishers Ltd. 1999)

Magnusson, Magnus (editor): *Chambers Biographical Dictionary* (1990)

Martin, Peter: *Samuel Johnson, a biography*
    (Weidenfield and Nicolson, 2008)

Mee, Arthur: *The King's England: Derbyshire*
    (Hodder & Stoughton 1937)

Nicholls, Graham: *A Guide to the Sameul Johnson Birthplace Museum,*
    Lichfield (1990)

Norman, John: *A Story of Breadsall Church* (1966, revised 1973)

Novak, Maximillian E.: *Daniel Defoe Master of Fictions* (OUP 2001)

Ollerenshaw, Arthur E.: *The History of Blue John Stone*

Oman, Carola: *The Wizard of the North. The Life of Sir Walter Scott*
    (Hodder and Stoughton 1973)

O'Neill, Jane: *The World of the Brontes* (Carlton 1997)

Ousby, Ian, Blue Guide.: *Literary. Britain and Ireland*
    (A&C Black Ltd. 1985)

Payne, C.J.: *Derby Churches Old and New and Derby's Golgotha*
    (Frank Murray 1893)

Pevsner, Nikolaus: *The Buildings of England. Derbyshire*
    (Penguin 1953)

Porter, Lindsey: *Castelton, Edale and Hathersage. Guide and Souvenir*
    (Ashbourne editions 2007)

Priestland, Neal: *Erasmus Darwin* (Ashbracken, Nottingham, 1990)

Redman, Nick: *An illustrated History of Breadsall Priory*
    (Marriott Hotels 2009)

Ripon, Nicola: *Derby Our City* (Breedon Books)

Shorter, Clement S.: *Charlotte Bronte and her circle*
  (Hodder and Stoughton, 1896)
Stafford, Fiona: *Brief Lives: Jane Austen* (Hesperus Press Ltd. 2008)
Taylor, Thomas: *A Life of Dr. Taylor* (St. Catherine's Press 1910)
The Peacock at Rowsley: A Short History published by the Hotel
Uttley, Alison: *Our Village* (Scarthin Books 1984
  for Alison Uttley Literary Property Trust, reprinted 2003)
Uttley, Alison: *The Country Child* (Faber and Faber 1931)
Vanson, Frederic: *A Pocket Dictionary of Derbyshire Place Names*
  (Hub 1973)
Wain, John: *Samuel Johnson* (Macmillan 1974)

A lane near Ashbourne

TRANSPORT

Each town and village mentioned in the book is accessible by public transport, either from Derby bus or train stations.

1. ASHBOURNE   Swift bus (Uttoxeter service) or 114 (less frequent)
2. BAKEWELL   Transpeak or 6.1 buses
3. BREADSALL   Y59 bus (Shipley View service)
4. CASTLETON   Hulleys 173 from Bakewell
5. CROMFORD   Transpeak or 6.1 buses. Train (Matlock service)
6. HATHERSAGE   Hulleys 271,272 from Bakewell (Sheffield service) .
Train from Derby to Hathersage, changing at Sheffield
7. MATLOCK BATH   Transpeak or 6.1 buses.
Train (Matlock service)
8. QUARNDON   114 bus (Ashbourne service)
9. ROWSLEY   Transpeak or 6.1 buses
10. WIRKSWORTH   6.1 bus
Train from Derby to Wirksworth, Derby to Matlock service (EMT), changing at Duffield to the Ecclesbourne Valley Railway (check local timetable)
6.1 service from Derby to Bakewell
Transpeak service from Derby to Buxton, or Derby to Manchester